T0286942

PRAISE FOR *A SPACE IN THE HEART*

"When my daughter recently asked me how my generation learned to handle life's punches, I responded flippantly that we'd find a sad song, listen to it on repeat for a week, and that usually did the trick. *A Space in the Heart* hits the exact same way. Larry Carlat walks through his loss with the honesty, vulnerability, and humility of a master lyricist, turning his deeply personal journey into our shared story of becoming Extraordinary Parents—from the moment everything turns black to the moment we discover we may just be able to enjoy the rest of our lives after all. Also: Wow. I loved it!" —**Jason Seiden**, co-founder of Comfort Communications. His daughter Elle died of suicide in 2018 after suffering from a long-term illness. She was fifteen.

"Rarely does a book elicit emotions the way *A Space in the Heart* does. Having gone through the death of my son and having read a lot of advice and personal histories on grieving, this book spoke to me more than any other. It felt like Larry was inside my head and heart. If you know anyone who has experienced this particular type of loss, his book will help strengthen your empathy and understand what otherwise seems beyond understanding." —**Vic Rauseo**, Emmy-award winning TV writer. His son Sam died of an overdose in 2018. He was twenty-seven.

"Larry Carlat does an impeccable job of telling the heartbreaking story of his beloved son's battle with alcohol, drugs, and mental illness, a story that ends in the horror of suicide. He does an equally compelling job of showing there is a way back from what feels like an endless nightmare and pain almost too great to bear. In a no-nonsense way, Carlat walks the griever down the long road that ultimately can lead a broken parent to once again find hope and joy in life." —**Susan Tick**, retired studio executive. Her daughter Molly died in 2020. An autopsy found no cause for her sudden death. She was twenty-nine.

"As someone whose son died by suicide, I've read many books focused on grief to try and help me grapple with this devastating loss. *A Space in the Heart* is one of the most valuable ones I've read on this topic. It's an honest and accurate portrayal of what so many parents feel in mourning their child while validating our thoughts and emotions along the way. Carlat is the perfect narrator, eloquently communicating the universal heartache that parents feel. I highly recommend this book, not only for parents who have lost a child, but for those eager to find the best ways to support them." —**Julie Halpert**, journalist and co-founder of the suicide prevention nonprofit, Garrett's Space. Her son Garrett took his own life in 2017. He was twenty-three.

"Larry Carlat guides you from the abyss of grief to a mountaintop where you can reclaim joy. There's no easy way to tell a story when it comes to the death of your child. Suicide makes it a double whammy. Society is often silent when it comes to a life taken by your child's own hand, but Larry is changing that with *A Space in the Heart*. Bereaved parents can find solace here as he provides the tools to emerge from the darkness fully transformed." —**Carla Kaufman Sloan**, Emmy-award-winning television writer. Her son Calder died in 2014 in an electrical accident in her home swimming pool. He was seven.

A Space in the Heart

A Survival Guide
for Grieving Parents

Larry Carlat

ROWMAN & LITTLEFIELD
Lanham • Boulder • New York • London

Published by Rowman & Littlefield
An imprint of The Rowman & Littlefield Publishing Group, Inc.
4501 Forbes Boulevard, Suite 200, Lanham, Maryland 20706
www.rowman.com

86-90 Paul Street, London EC2A 4NE

Distributed by NATIONAL BOOK NETWORK

British Library Cataloguing in Publication Information Available

Library of Congress Cataloging-in-Publication Data

Names: Carlat, Larry, author.
Title: A space in the heart : a survival guide for grieving parents / Larry
    Carlat.
Description: Lanham : Rowman & Littlefield, [2025] | Summary: "A Space in
    the Heart: A Survival Guide for Grieving Parents expresses the anguish
    of the death of a child and offers hope for how to survive and thrive in
    its aftermath. Part memoir, part self-help, zero bullshit, and 100
    percent from the heart, it confronts our never-ending love for our
    children and how that love helps us transform and heal"— Provided by
    publisher.
Identifiers: LCCN 2024021794 (print) | LCCN 2024021795 (ebook) | ISBN
    9781538186596 (cloth) | ISBN 9781538186602 (ebook)
Subjects: LCSH: Parental grief. | Children—Death.
Classification: LCC BF575.G7 C373 2025 (print) | LCC BF575.G7 (ebook) |
    DDC 155.9/37085—dc23/eng/20240603
LC record available at https://lccn.loc.gov/2024021794
LC ebook record available at https://lccn.loc.gov/2024021795

∞™ The paper used in this publication meets the minimum requirements of
American National Standard for Information Sciences—Permanence of Paper
for Printed Library Materials, ANSI/NISO Z39.48-1992.

For Caryn and Zach

I have a space in my heart that never closes.

—Robbie James Carlat, age seven

Contents

Part III: The Beginning

Preface

$\mathcal{I}$'m sorry.

I'm sorry for your loss.

I'm sorry for the agony you're in.

I'm sorry you're reading this book right now.

Even though we've never met before, I know a few things about you: I know you're in the worst pain you've ever felt in your life. I know you can't stop crying. I know you may have thought about not being here anymore. I know there are no words that can make you feel any better.

I know these things because I am you. I am you in the future. I am you a few years down the road, once you make it through to the other side of where you're going. Right now, you have no idea where you're going, which is where I come in.

I'm here to gently guide you and hold space for you. I've been where you are, and I'm honored to take your hand and walk through the darkness as you slowly move toward the light. I know it sounds strange, but we are connected. We are connected by our common loss and our uncommon pain. We are connected by our extraordinariness. You'll find out what I mean by that as we make our journey together.

In the meantime, I'd like to share a few things I think you should know about me. The first thing is I'm not a psychologist, social worker, or trauma expert, although I am a grief counselor and coach. I volunteer as a group leader for bereaved parents at Our House Grief Support Center in Los Angeles, I sit on its board of directors, and I created a grief coaching site called Grief for Guys. I'm also a writer and an editor, but more than anything, I'm a father who is compelled to help others who, like me, have lost a child they loved.

I'd love to tell you that the reason I poured out what was left of my heart was to help other parents who might one day find themselves bereft, but that thought didn't even cross my mind until I was more than halfway through documenting my own year of magical thinking. It happened one night, near the end of a meeting of my grief group, when one of my fellow distraught parents said, "No one can prepare you for this, but I wish there was a book or manual that would help guide us through the sadness." That's when I decided I'd write one for her and for all the future members of the world's worst club.

The second thing you should know is that I don't pull any punches. The last thing I want to do is add to your anguish, because I know that pain all too well. But I won't sugarcoat things and tell you that everything is going to be all right. Maybe it will or maybe it won't; that will be entirely up to you. What I will tell you is that grief isn't something you overcome—but you can learn to live with it.

I have and you can too.

That's what *A Space in the Heart* is really about. It's about the anguish caused by the death of a child and how to survive and thrive afterward. It's part memoir, part self-help, zero bullshit, and 100 percent straight from the heart. It's about our never-ending love for our lost children and how that love ultimately helps us transform and heal. In other words, it's a road map for a road no one would ever choose to travel.

One of the many other things I learned is that grief lasts until the day we die. The questions become: What do we want to do with it until then? And how do we want to live our lives knowing that we've lost a vital piece of who we are? My greatest wish is that this book will help answer those existential questions and, above all, provide unwavering hope along the way.

My older son Rob took his own life in February 2019. He was twenty-eight. He suffered from depression, bipolar disorder, and alcoholism. He also had conflicted feelings about being adopted. Twenty-five years ago, I wrote a letter to Robbie (he was Robbie back then) about my own conflicted feelings about adopting him for *Esquire* magazine. I think that's a good place to start. You'll be hearing plenty more about Rob—as well as all you need to know about the mind-, heart-, and soul-bending journey ahead of you—in the chapters to come.

∽

Dear Robbie,

You were born a poet. Let me quote a few of your best lines:
I bet my birth mother is still crying.
I wish God would take the sadness off me.
If she kept me, I never would've known you.
I have a space in my heart that never closes.
As I sit here wrestling with words that invariably elude my grasp, I wish I could write like that. But what do I expect? You are seven and I am only forty-two.

Before you read any further, you should know that your mom doesn't want me to write this. She doesn't want me to write anything that might one day awaken any doubt in you. So I made a deal with her. I promised that if she feels the same way after I've finished, I'll punt on the whole thing. That's how intensely she feels about you, how fiercely protective she is of you. She doesn't want me to write this letter because she loves you so much and I love you so much that I have to write it, even if I don't show it to you until you have kids of your own.

Here are the words your mom fears: *I didn't want to adopt you.*

I know that sounds like powerful stuff, but to me those words are as trifling as the ants that march across our kitchen floor before you put your thumb to them. They mean nothing because I can't even remember feeling that way. I've searched my heart and can't find any trace of not wanting you. It would be like not wanting air. Still, just as I can't imagine not wanting you now, there was a time that I couldn't imagine *you.* I didn't know you were going to be you. I only knew you were not going to be *me.*

Your mom says I was hung up on this crazy little thing called genetics, which should never be mistaken for that crazy little thing called love. It all seems so bizarre, given that my family background includes everything from cancer and heart disease to criminal behavior. Your mom says that I was worried that you wouldn't be perfect, that we would be inheriting somebody else's problem, and that nurture would be revealed as nothing more than nature's cheap consolation prize. Your mom says I can't recollect any of these gory details because sometimes I can be a stubborn bastard.

That must be where you get it from.

Because, Rob, when all is said and done, you are me—only way better looking. You are me, if I looked like Brad Pitt and your mom looked like Sharon Stone. You're more like me than Zachary, who inherited torn genes from me and Mom. You and I are both the eldest son, moderately shy, and exceedingly anxious. We love Michael Jordan, movies, scallion pancakes, and the occasional doody joke. We're natural-born outsiders who share the same thin skin.

And there's something else that you and I have in common: I once had a space in my heart that wouldn't close. I still remember the cause. When I was four years old, two very large men wearing very large hats came into our house and took my father away. He didn't come back for eight years, and even when he returned, he couldn't repair what had been ripped apart. My dad, like yours, was a sad schmuck, sad in that he never tried to change himself into a dad.

For me, everything changed the moment I saw you.

After four years of infertility and a bout with cancer thrown in for good luck (if I hadn't had it, I never would have known you), I was finally ready to entertain alternatives to producing a mirror image. I tend to arrive at places in my heart long after your mom has moved in and decorated. Your mom always knew that she wanted to be a mom, while I was just beginning to understand what it meant to be a dad. You know the next part from your baby book that you keep under your pillow:

> They met a wonderful young lady who was growing a baby boy in her belly. But she wasn't able to give her baby all the good things the world had to offer, and she wanted that for him very, very much.

Seven months later, I found myself in the hospital scanning the blue "It's a Boy!" stickers on the bassinets until I saw your birth mother's last name neatly printed in black ink. And at that moment, the space in my heart was filled. It was either magic or God; I've forgotten what I believed in at the time. "You're my son; you're my son," I quietly mouthed to you through the glass again and again, trying to convince myself that you were real. Then I went to your mom and we hugged and cried, while you kept sleeping, our little boy, Robbie James Carlat, unaware of how much joy you could bring to two people.

And the reason I can no longer recall not wanting to adopt you is simple: that feeling completely vanished on the day you were born. "I know, I know. It was love at first sight," you like to say, sounding like a cartoon version of me anytime I bring up the subject of your birth. But it wasn't like that between my dad and me. I don't remember my father ever kissing me or, for that matter, me kissing him. The thought of saying "I love you" to each other, even when he came back from jail or as he lay dying, would have cracked both of us up. In fact, the closest my father ever came to a term of endearment was calling me "Kiddo" (which is the full extent of his paternal legacy and why I usually answer "Ditto, Kiddo" when you say "I love you").

There's a black-and-white photograph of my dad holding me high above his head—I must have been six months old—and it's the only time I can recall him looking genuinely happy to be with me. I used to think of that picture in the months after you were born when I danced you to sleep. I never dance, not even with your mom ("They're all going to laugh at you!" from *Carrie* pretty much sums up why), but I loved dancing with you. While you sucked on your bottle, I savored the feeling of your tiny heartbeat against my own. Joni Mitchell's *Night Ride Home* CD was on just loud enough so we wouldn't wake up your mom, and I'd gently sing to you, "All we ever wanted, was just to come in from the cold, come in, come in, come in from the cold."

Still, the space you were coming in from was far colder than mine had ever been. It's the original black hole, and all of our kissing and hugging are not enough. All of your incessant *I love yous* and *I love the familys*—words you repeated as if to convince yourself, the same way I did when I first set eyes on you—are not enough. All of the times that you asked me to pick you up—and I happily obliged because I knew a day would come when you would stop asking—are not enough. Every night when we read your baby book, which desperately tries to explain whose belly you grew in and how you got to us, is not enough.

Nothing is enough, for there's nothing that approaches the clear and direct poetry of "I hate myself because I'm adopted" or "I'm only happy when I'm hugging and kissing you. All the other times I just make-believe." If anything, you get the prize for coming closest to the pin with, "Being adopted is hard to understand." And what do you win for saying the darndest things? A profound sadness. And let's not forget its little brother, anger, which you direct at your little brother for no apparent reason other than that he serves as a constant reminder that you are the one who is not like the others.

The irony is that Zachy, the prototypical little bro, only wants to be you, while you'd do anything to be him.

I hope that one day God grants your wish and takes the sadness from you, because your mom and I know how truly blessed we are to have two beautiful sons—one chosen by us and one chosen for us. It's like we wrote at the end of your baby book:

Mommy and Daddy waited a long time for a baby—a baby boy just like you. And though it might have been nice to have you grow in mommy's belly . . . always remember that you grew in our hearts!

Perhaps the only thing we neglected to consider at the time was *your* heart. Which reminds me of sandcastles. A few summers ago, you and I built a beauty on Uncle Stephen's beach, and you wanted to surround it with a moat, so we started to dig a hole with your big yellow bucket. We kept digging faster and faster until the hole got so deep that you jumped in. "Daddy, get the water," you said, and I ran into the waves, filled the bucket, dragged it back, and dumped it into the hole. The sand quickly drank it up, so I kept going back and forth, trying to fill the hole with water, but it was like pouring the water down a drain, and after a while we finally said "to hell with it" and ran into the ocean.

You are the sand, little boy, and I will always be the water.

And that was where I intended to end this letter until you came padding into the room in your G.I. Joe pajamas.

"What are you writing about?" you asked.

And when I told you it was a story about you, you asked, "Is it going to be in a big magazine?"

And I said, "Yeah, how do you feel about that?"

And you said, "Scared."

And I said, "How come?"

And you said, "Because I'm going to be in it alone."

And I said, "No, you won't. I'll be in it with you."

And you said, "I love you, daddy."

And that's when I had to stop writing.

Part I

THE END

A Day in the Life . . .
If You Can Still Call It That

*Y*ou wake up in the morning and for the first few hazy seconds, you think maybe it was all a bad dream. As soon as you get out of bed, a tidal wave of grief knocks you down, bringing you to your knees, and you immediately start to cry. You can't stop crying. This is the beginning of the end of your life as you knew it—grieving your child who is no longer alive. Whether it was a long goodbye, a short goodbye, or no goodbye, you want the pain to stop but you don't think it ever will.

How could it? How will you go on? *Why* should you go on? Everything has turned to shit. Things will never be the same. You will never be the same. Your child has died and a part of you has, too. Your world has gone from color to black and white, though it's mostly just pitch black. The light—your darling son, your beautiful daughter—is gone forever and you're left alone, stumbling in the dark.

You drag yourself into the shower and try to wash the anguish away. You scrub and scrub until it hurts and then you scrub some more until you burst out crying again. The shower is one of the few refuges where you can let go, where you can turn your insides out. The shower cleanses your body but can't purify your soul.

You get dressed, unaware that you're wearing two different colored shoes, and look in the mirror to see if you're still in one piece. It surprises you that you are. But there's something different about your eyes. They're dull and lifeless, like one of those zombies on *The Walking Dead*. You wonder if people can see the sorrow in your eyes, or the hole in your heart, or the bottomless pit in your stomach, and then you wonder if they can see you at all.

You eat a light breakfast because the barely rational part of you knows that you need to keep up your strength, but everything tastes awful. Really, everything has no taste at all. You have no appetite for anything—least of all, for your life.

The phone rings and you jump out of your skin before realizing that there's no longer a reason to ever do that again. You still have the coroner's voicemail to prove it. This time, it's just a little PTSD calling to say hello.

You hop in the car and begin to cry again because this is your other fortress of solitude. You think this is where you do your best crying—the deep, guttural, ugly kind that barely sounds human. This is the start of your mourning commute.

Your first stop is your therapist's office. Today she wants you to recall the moment you got the horrible phone call because that's part of the EMDR (eye movement desensitization and reprocessing) therapy, which supposedly will help you to rewire your trauma and relieve your emotional distress. As your eyes begin to track her hand as she moves it in and out of your field of vision while you're tapping your fingers on your legs, you think, *Am I the biggest idiot for doing this ridiculous thing? Or am I just that desperate to make the sadness subside?* When she finally says your time is up, you curse God for saying the same to your child.

When you get to work, everyone is extra-nice yet a little skittish about approaching you. When they do pay their condolences, it's awkward (*"There are no words"*), and you say thank you and smile politely, and a colleague gives you a big hug. Hugs have never felt so soothing before, and you don't want to let go—not just because it feels good but also because you need to feel connected. The physical contact reminds you that you're still a part of this world, an unjust world without your child.

Your cell phone buzzes again, and you feel the same sickening jolt in your belly. *When will this stop?* you think, and this time it's your best friend checking in to see if you're "all right." You hate those words. Nothing will ever be "all right." Right now, everything is all wrong—with no end in sight. *Why can't everyone just leave me the hell alone?* you think, and then you thank your best friend for calling.

You throw yourself into your work, hoping it will be a distraction, and it goes pretty well for a while until something reminds you of your child and reduces you to a puddle. You run to the bathroom before anyone can see you and lock yourself behind a stall. When someone walks in, you bite down hard on your hand, hoping to silence your sobs.

After a productive morning of mourning, it's time for lunch, and your best work friend wants to take you out, so you slip on your "all right" mask and prepare to be peppered with the same questions that everyone keeps asking. They're all variations on "How are you doing?" and you wonder for a second, *Should I really tell this person how I'm feeling? Does this person really want to hear that my guts have been ripped out and how badly I'm suffering every second, minute, hour of every day?* Instead, you say, "I'm hanging in there, doing the best I can," and they smile and nod approvingly.

They actually look a little relieved because they really don't want to hear about your agony, and you really don't want to inflict it upon them. How can they possibly understand what you're going through anyway? You can barely comprehend it yourself. So you quietly eat your tasteless salad and make small talk until the check arrives. Your best work friend is happy to pick it up, and you think that one of the few fringe benefits of having a dead kid is all the free meals you've been getting lately.

The afternoon crawls by, and you picture yourself in this metaphor, crawling on all fours while caught in rush hour traffic on the way home. *Home.* Home used to be one of your favorite words. Home is where the people you love most in the world live. Except for one of them. Now you have to face your husband, wife, or partner, and, in many cases, your other children, and it's your job to comfort them, to reassure them, to hold on to them for dear life.

After dinner, when everyone has retreated to wherever they go to lick their wounds, you crack open what has become a nightly bottle of wine and pour yourself a hefty glass. You plunk down on the couch and hope that maybe by the time you finish the bottle, your heartache will ease a tiny bit. Maybe you'll finally get a good night's sleep. Maybe you won't wake up tomorrow. Maybe you'll drown yourself in more maybes, you think.

You turn on some mindless TV show, because that's all you can handle right now and you're not really watching anyway; it's just random images and background noise that complement the mayhem of your thoughts. And it comes as no surprise that you're crying again, even though you're watching Guy Fieri eating cheeseburger fried rice on Food Network, so you pour yourself another tall glass and head into the bedroom.

Your husband or wife is already zonked out, so you decide to skim one of the many grief books people have recommended, but everything you read just makes you feel worse. Finally, you pop a Xanax or two, turn off the lights, and try to go to sleep.

And that's when things get really dark, because now it's just you and the relentless voices in your head. You're trying to make sense of something that doesn't make sense, and yet you keep trying because you think it will provide relief, connecting the dots, explaining the unexplainable, hoping against hope that you can miraculously change the outcome. You hope that somehow this will make the pain go away, knowing full well that nothing can ever take it away, knowing that the pain will last forever.

It's a grotesque feedback loop in which you're stuck inside your own head and the walls are filled with pictures of your child, and wherever you look, there's your kid looking back at you, sometimes smiling, sometimes sad, sometimes angry, sometimes completely expressionless, but always looking you directly in the eye. And you want to hold them and shake them and hug them and kiss them, and more than anything, you want to hear their voice, you want to hear them laugh or curse or say, "I love you," but they can't speak because it's just pictures.

So you dig a little deeper, looking for memories that come with their own soundtrack, and you think you can hear them, but really it's just you putting words in their mouth—*I love you, Mom; I love you, Dad; I love you; I love you; I love you*—over and over until it's just a faint whisper, and even though you're wide awake, it feels like a horrible dream and you just want it to end. You keep saying it was just a bad dream, it was just a bad dream, it was just a bad dream, the same thing you told your child when they were having one.

Then you take a deep breath and dry your eyes. You didn't even realize that you were crying again—when will you ever stop crying?—and now you're just sitting in bed and looking at a photo of your daughter or son on the nightstand, the one from a million years ago before you got the phone call that irrevocably changed your life. You can see their exquisite beauty and feel their divine spirit, and you say out loud *Why? Why? Why? Why?* And they look right back at you—the most beautiful child in the world—and they don't say a word.

You wake up the next morning and once again, for the first few seconds, you think maybe it was all a bad dream. This is now your life—if you can still call it that—when your child's life ends.

• 2 •

My Bad Dream

*P*hew! That was a lot, I know. But what you're going through is a lot, and I know you know that too. Now for some good news (yes, there's good news!): this is a bad dream you can wake up from. It will take time. It will take work. It will take pain. It will take strength. It will take an open heart. It will take everything you have. It will take things you didn't know you have. As I said and will continue to repeat throughout this book, grief isn't something that you conquer . . . but you can learn to live with it. You can learn to live with sorrow and joy. Right now, it's all sorrow, but that will change.

I promise.

My bad dream began when I saw Rob the day before he killed himself.

We were going to have lunch, and I called him when I pulled up to his apartment in Long Beach, California. "Yo," he answered groggily, like he had just woken up.

"Yo, I'm downstairs. Thought maybe we can go to Din Tai Fung for soup dumplings," I said. "It's a little bit of a hike, but I don't have to be anywhere."

"I don't know if I have enough time to do it today," he said, "but I'll be down in a minute."

By the time Rob got into my car, he had changed his mind, so we headed to the Del Amo mall in Torrance. I hadn't seen him in a few weeks, as I was amid something called "detaching with love," a coping strategy my ex-wife Caryn learned and passed along to me from her

Families Anonymous meetings. Rob had long been an unreliable narrator, and his latest story was a doozy about owing back rent and borrowing thousands of dollars from a loan shark who had threatened him with bodily harm if he was late with his payments. There was always a germ of truth in Rob's stories, and this one involved even more disturbing details, but I was going through some of my own shit at the time, mainly looking for a new job, and I just couldn't deal with more of his.

I started to bombard him with the usual questions—most importantly, what was going on at his jobs. He was bouncing around between a few short-order cooking gigs, and I knew he wasn't sleeping much, which had become fairly typical for Rob. For the past year, he'd been working the graveyard shift as a food and beverage supervisor at a run-down casino (not the ideal gig for someone in recovery). So he was pretty much always just waking up whenever I saw him for lunch.

"Dad, can we pass on the job interview today?" he asked, annoyed. "I really don't feel like talking about it. This is my one break from all that shit, so let's just talk about something else."

We were both quiet for the rest of the ride. He was on his phone, reading through his Reddit feed, while I was thinking of things not to say.

We slipped into a more familiar routine as soon as we sat down at the table. Rob began to fill in the menu ticket without even asking, just like we always did it—three orders of pork soup dumplings, fried pork chop, chicken fried noodles, a lemon iced tea for me and a strawberry mango slush smoothie for him. It sounds like a lot of food, but we always polished it off. Everything seemed normal. It was just another unremarkable day hanging out together.

We shot the shit like we always did, and the only piece of pertinent information I remember is him talking about the navy. His friend had recently enlisted and Rob was thinking of doing the same. He went as far as taking a psych eval but failed because of his 5150 hold from the previous year, when he was suicidal and admitted for a three-day psychiatric evaluation. As I sit here writing these words, it's easy to see how desperate he was to find an escape.

When we got back to his apartment building, I said we'd talk soon and fist-bumped him. Then he said the words he always said when I dropped him off, my favorite four words in the world, the last words he ever said to me: "I love you, Dad."

The phone call came at 4:18 a.m. on Thursday, February 6, while I was fast asleep, which is unusual for me because I'm the world's lightest sleeper—and I had been waiting for the call for more than ten years. I woke up at about 7:00 and saw that I had a voicemail message from an LA number. It's funny how I don't even listen to voicemail anymore, I just read the transcription, and as I scanned a few key words—investigator, born January 18, 1991, reference case number—I knew.

I knew this day was coming. I didn't know when, I didn't know that it would be the day after we had lunch together. I didn't know it would be like this, but I knew. I had known for a very long time.

Whenever I saw Caryn's name come up on my phone, my heart would beat out of my chest, fearing the worst. It was the same for her when she saw that I was calling. Certainly we'd had more than our share of horrifying phone calls through the years. In recent times, I would text Caryn before calling to ease her mind that there was nothing bad going on with Rob, to let her know in advance that I just wanted to say hi.

I went downstairs to grab a cup of coffee before returning the call. I was strangely calm and I'm still not sure exactly why. The fog of shock hadn't yet sunk in; it was more a mixture of heartbreak and resignation. Those first few moments felt like time had stopped.

"He's either dead or in jail," I said to my girlfriend Maura, who was immediately panic-stricken.

I listened to the message, and it began with a too-friendly "Hi," which is an immediate tip-off that you're about to leave the worst message in the world.

"My name is Jennifer Herzog. I'm an investigator with Los Angeles County," she began as her voice started to flatten out. "I'm looking for family for Robbie James Carlat, born January 18, 1991. If you know Robbie, can you please give me a call back."

I know Robbie, I thought.

· 3 ·

Gentle on My Mind

*W*hatever you're feeling right now is what you should be feeling right now. If you're sad and depressed, fine. If you're often angry, good. If you can't feel anything, well, that's okay too. If you're stressed, worried, and feeling all the feels, so be it. There's no wrong way to feel about losing your child. You can't fuck it up any worse than it already is.

As if that isn't hard enough, you're probably beating up yourself. Don't worry, we all do it. It's the most natural response to the most unnatural disaster a parent can possibly experience. Guilt, shame, regret—pick your poison. You torture yourself thinking about something you could have done to prevent the whole mess. *Slap!* You're tormented about all the wrong things you've said and all the right things you should've said. *Smack!* Your relentless guilt tells you that you deserve the pain because you've failed miserably at the most fundamental aspect of being a parent: protecting your child. *Pow!* You beat the living daylights out of yourself because you're still living and your child will never see daylight again. *Oomph!*

It's all perfectly normal, although those two words couldn't feel any further from what you're currently going through—and we'll get back to what you're "going through" later on, when you realize that's what you've been doing.

In the meantime, I'm going to tell you something that is way easier said than done, that sounds so obvious and simplistic that when you hear it, you'll nod in agreement, although you won't be able to do it until you're ready to do it. Here it is: *be gentle with yourself.*

I first heard those words at the end of the first grief group I ever attended. I had been beating myself up with all kinds of excruciating questions: How can I reconcile eating soup dumplings with Rob in the afternoon and him taking his own life the next night? How do you love someone with all of your heart even though he keeps breaking it over and over again? How do you save someone who doesn't want to be saved? I finally let myself off the hook when I asked one last question: how can I be so furious about what he did when I know that it wasn't him but his mental illness that made him do it?

Mental illness was the only thing that made sense of Rob's death. Rob was sick, and when the sick part took over his life, he finally decided to do something about it and checked out. When I came to that realization, I stopped punishing myself and never looked back.

So now the question is: what's it going to take for *you*?

YOU: I don't know. All I do is cry. I can't stop.

ME: Crying is good for you. It may not feel good—actually, I know from experience that it feels like sheer pain—but it will feel good down the road.

YOU: I don't know if anything will ever feel good again. How can it? I feel so broken. There's a piece of me that is missing—it's gone and can never be replaced. How can I be gentle with myself when I don't feel like myself?

ME: Good question. Let me reassure you: you are yourself. You don't feel like yourself because you're at *the end* right now—the end of who you were. Soon you'll be going through *the middle*—that's where a transformation takes place—and eventually, in your own time and in your own way, you'll arrive at *the beginning* of who you have become: an extraordinary parent. The pain of losing a child never really goes away, but it does lessen as you learn to integrate it into your life.

YOU: I want to believe you, I really do, but I'm hurting right now like I've never hurt before. I feel the pain of missing my kid. And then I feel like it's all my fault. Like how could I have allowed this to happen? This isn't supposed to happen. This isn't supposed to happen to me. What did I do to deserve this?

ME: You don't deserve this and it's not your fault.

YOU: Thank you for saying that, but I'll never forgive myself, which makes me so mad. I walk around feeling mad all the time. I'm mad at my child. I'm mad at the world. I'm mad at God. I feel like I'm going mad.

ME: Well, this is where "be gentle with yourself" comes in handy. The pain, as I vividly remember it, is so intense and unrelenting and yet, at the same time, necessary. It's necessary in helping you process the loss while keeping you connected to your child. What's not necessary are the self-inflicted wounds. The ones we torture ourselves with, the ones that keep us up all night, the ones that cut the deepest.

YOU: I know you're giving me helpful advice and I appreciate it, truly, but sometimes I just can't get out of my own way. The questions—the whys, the what-ifs—fly in from nowhere and it's just so easy to tumble down that rabbit hole and punish myself. It's hard to separate, much less distinguish, the pain and heartbreak of my child's death from the pain and guilt I'm inflicting on myself.

ME: Let's try a little experiment: Close your eyes and think about your best friend. Can you picture them? Good! Now think about a time when they might have been going through a particularly rough patch in their life. Maybe it was a health scare or a marriage crisis or a serious problem at work—something that was troubling at their core. Or maybe, God forbid a million times, imagine they're going through what you're going through right now.

YOU: God forbid a million times.

ME: And your best friend calls you one day because they're at the end of their rope and need to confide in someone who will understand what they're feeling. They need to feel connected to someone who gets them, someone who can tell them they're not crazy, someone who has always given them sound advice.

That someone is *you*.

Your friend starts out sobbing, revealing their darkest thoughts about the death of their child, and just as you said before, they're feeling guilty and angry and scared and confused and mad at the world, and they also share something they have never shared with anyone else, something that makes them feel like a monster. Your friend tells you that they feel relieved because they've been waiting for that nightmarish phone call for a long time. They say that it feels like they finally stopped holding their breath, and, ironically, that deepens their guilt and suffering even more. Your friend goes on to confess that the only reason they're still here is for the sake of their other children. And after all is said and done, they circle back to blaming themselves for their child's death.

YOU: Oh my God! I wouldn't wish that kind of heartbreak on anyone.

ME: Your best friend is in the worst pain imaginable. Only you, of course, can imagine it, because you've been there and want to help any way you can. You're listening with all of your heart, and finally it's your turn to speak. What do you say?

YOU: Wow! Whew! Gimme a second here. That was a lot. Um . . . the first thing I would tell them is that I love them.

ME: Good start.

YOU: Then I would say it again and again, and we'd both start to cry, just like I'm crying now. And I'd tell them that they're not to blame and to stop beating themselves up about it because they're the best parent I've ever known, and they did everything in their power to save their child. And I'd tell them that I've always admired their courage, their strength, and their perseverance. And I'd remind my friend that it wasn't their fault because they did the best they could, and I'd tell them that they could ask all the whys and what-ifs from now until the end of time and it's never going to bring their child back. Then maybe I'd suggest they stop torturing themselves because the pain of losing their child is unbearable enough. It doesn't need any reinforcement, particularly when the thoughts in their head aren't true, and I'd keep reminding them how much I love them and how much they need to love and—you bastard!—I'd tell them: *be gentle with yourself!*

ME: Bravo! And? . . .

YOU: And that I should probably extend the same loving kindness to myself! *Ha!* I see what you did there, dude!

ME: I'm glad you did! It's such an important reminder. Your grief deserves your compassion. Your heart is broken, but there's still room in there to love yourself.

YOU: I just miss my baby so much.

ME: You know they're with you. They'll always be with you.

YOU: You're making me cry again.

ME: Well, now, let's see if I can possibly make you smile.

• *4* •

One from the Heart

*L*et's step out from the darkness for just a moment and take a walk into the light. I want you to think of a sweet memory of your child from back in the day—one from the heart, a memory that makes you smile.

I know there's a good chance you're not ready to take in any type of happiness just yet. In fact, you may not be ready to do much of anything about your grief this early on, which is common and understandable. If this sounds like you, maybe dog-ear this page for now and return a little later, because I can guarantee your feelings will change.

I also realize this moment of bliss is now a double-edged sword that can also slice you open, but it's important to focus on the good times we had with our children, even if it doesn't always feel so good. We need to keep these happy memories alive.

I was about to suggest you start with a sort of time travel, but as I began to type those words, it took me back to a few weeks after Rob was born, so I guess I'll go first. We had this great party in our apartment in Forest Hills, New York, and invited all of our friends and family to help us celebrate his arrival. We sent out invitations that said, "You are invited to the debut performance of Robbie James Carlat in *It's a Wonderful Life.*" And on that day, it certainly was.

I remember only bits and pieces, but every memory makes me smile. I was floating from person to person, hugging and kissing everyone, introducing friends to my other friends, and ushering people into our bedroom to meet the little man of the hour, who was in Caryn's arms, wrapped tightly in a tie-dyed blankie, absolutely clueless about the festivities in his honor. Except for the days that he and Zach were born, I can't remember ever being happier in my life.

15

Maybe you were lucky enough to have so many idyllic memories and happy days with your child that it's difficult to pick just one, or maybe you're more like me and had them few and far between. Whatever your circumstance, here are a few gentle reminders and some ways to best keep your children in your heart.

Remember one of their first birthdays when you had to help blow out the candles? *Picture their angelic, smiling face, close your eyes, and softly blow one out for them right now.*

Remember teaching them to ride a bike and how terrified you both were to let go until the moment that you did, and they started to ride all by themselves, and you were both relieved and ecstatic? *Hop on your bike this weekend and bring your child along for the ride.*

Remember building a sandcastle at the beach and asking them to fill up a pail with water, and by the time they carried it back to you, there was hardly any water left in the pail, so you decided to hunt for cool shells and shiny rocks instead, and after a few more minutes, you both ran into the ocean and immediately got pummeled by a wave? *Take a walk on the beach and hunt for shiny rocks. When you find a good one, bring it home and place it where you can see it every day.*

Remember taking your child to their first baseball game, when you had great box seats because a friend had season tickets, and your kid brought along their glove hoping to catch a foul ball, and they didn't care that it didn't happen because they ate five or six hot dogs on that steamy July afternoon, and you both had a great time even though you left in the fifth inning because you both thought the game itself was boring, and on the way out of the stadium you bought a hot pretzel for the long car ride home? *Go to a baseball game (let's go Mets!), buy yourself a cold beer, pour one out for your homie, and then leave in the fifth inning because the game will be boring.*

Remember going to Disney World with your child, waiting in long lines to go on all of the classic rides and finishing the day at Splash Mountain, sitting in the front of the log flume together as you drifted in the dark river wending its way up to the top of the hill, and you were both a little creeped out by the animatronic characters and you were both a little scared to take the plunge, so you held hands when it was your turn at the top, and you both screamed and laughed and screamed some more when the log began to drop, and they snapped a photo of the two of you, and *you* were the one with your eyes closed? *Find that photo in the old shoebox in the back of your closet, close your eyes, and let out a small scream.*

Remember playing hide-and-seek, pretending you couldn't see them under the bed or behind a curtain or in the back of a closet and stomping around and stage-whispering something like, "I wonder where Robbie is? I wonder where he could be?" Then you'd look under the bed or pull back the curtain or open the closet door and shout, "There he is!" and you'd both crack up, and it was your turn to hide? *Open a hall closet and quietly say, "There he is!"*

Remember when your child danced around maniacally in the living room to one of your favorite songs (in our house it was "Wonderwall" by Oasis and R.E.M.'s "It's the End of the World as We Know It . . . And I Feel Fine")? Maybe you had a puppy who joined in the merriment, and you started to dance along with them, and you were both giggling because it was so much fun crazy-dancing together? *Blast your favorite song and dance like no one's watching, although you know your special someone is.*

Remember watching a movie together that you both loved (it was *Monty Python and the Holy Grail* for me and Rob, but I'm guessing that's not a universal choice), making Jiffy Pop, plopping down on the couch in the den, and reciting your favorite lines from the movie? Then they'd want to watch it again, so you rewound the VHS tape and about fifteen minutes in (right after the Black Knight says the immortal line, "It's just a flesh wound!"), they'd fall asleep in your arms, and have you ever seen a more beautiful child in your entire life? *Whatever that movie was for you, find it on your favorite streaming service and watch it until you fall asleep.*

Remember reading them a bedtime story, and how delicious their head smelled right after coming out of the bath, and how they were wearing their G.I. Joe pajamas and wouldn't let you leave their room until you read one more book, Daddy, please? *Pick up* Goodnight Moon *or* Harold and the Purple Crayon *or whatever book your child loved best and read it out loud every night for a week, and just before you nod out, remember to say good night to your child.* "Good night, Rob," *I've whispered every night since he died.*

Remember the last time they gave you a big hug—one of those embraces that feels like your hearts are touching—and then said, "I love you"? *Hold on tight to that memory and never let it go.*

• 5 •

It's Not about the Words

I've come to hate the words *there are no words*, mainly because so many people said exactly those words to me when Rob died. It amazes me that people used words to say that there aren't any. I knew what they were trying to convey—that it's impossible to articulate the depth of their sadness or to imagine the unimaginable heartache of losing a child. I get it because I used to be one of those people.

I never knew the right thing to say and trying always made me squirrelly. It still does, and that's after Rob has been dead and buried for more than five years. After reading a ton of books on grief and consulting ChatGPT, I know that "I'm sorry for your loss" is the go-to sentiment on the menu of comforting responses to say to someone who has lost a loved one, followed by "If there's anything I can do, don't hesitate to ask." Whenever someone said that to me, I always wanted to answer, "Paint my house!"—the punchline to one of my father-in-law's favorite old jokes. (RIP, Mart!)

My friend Steve, whose son Gabe died of an accidental overdose a few years ago, sometimes helps people out with their commiseration attempts by cutting them off before things get too awkward. He calls this play an "interception."

"I'm going to stop you right there," he'll say, "I appreciate your kind condolences" and then he'll nod curtly, signaling an end to the conversation.

The truth is, it's not about the words. The truth is, we don't really care what you say. I take that back. We actually do care . . . but whatever you say will invariably annoy the hell out of us. It's not you; it's us. We can't hear the words because we're in severe emotional pain, and you can't understand our pain because no one can understand unless you have a dead child, so shut the fuck up with your "I'm so sorrys" and your "there are no words."

We know you mean well, we really do, but now we have to pretend to be gracious and appreciative of your kindness. I know that sounds shitty and ungrateful, but this is really how we feel when we hear whatever it is that's coming out of your mouth. To us it sounds like the muffled trombone voices of the adults in a surreal Peanuts cartoon called *Your Kid Just Died, Charlie Brown.*

It all boils down to one immutable thing: there's nothing you can say that takes our pain away. So now what?

Start with a hug. I can still feel the hugs I got after Rob died. When I hugged my dear friends Tony and Gina, I felt them take me into their hearts. It was what I needed and continued to need. If a picture is worth a thousand words, a hug is worth a million. Maybe I love hugs so much because Rob gave the best hugs, and I miss them almost as much as I miss him.

Perhaps the best and most loving thing you can do for someone who is grieving is to listen to them. That's what we need the most, particularly when it's fresh and impossible to process anything because everything feels so empty and meaningless, especially words.

Just listen to us with an open heart and mind. Listen to us with no judgment. Listen to us when we can barely speak. There's a lot going on in our silence. "There are no words" doesn't mean there are no feelings, but there are times that those feelings can be so immense that they should never be put into words.

I never struggled with words in my life until I made the two most difficult phone calls ever to my ex-wife and son, telling them that Rob had killed himself.

"I have terrible news," I said to Caryn. "I just got the phone call."

"Which one?" she asked, bracing herself for one of the only two possibilities we ever discussed.

"Rob's dead. He killed himself."

All I remember after saying the words I had feared saying since Rob was a teenager is hearing Caryn cry like I've never heard anyone cry before. I would try to describe the sound to you, but nothing's coming to me.

"I know, I know," I mindlessly repeated over and over again as I listened to her wail in agony. I remained calm but couldn't think of anything else to say.

After a few minutes, I told her everything that the coroner and the police had told me and then we talked about telling Zach.

"Don't call him at work," Caryn said. "Wait until he gets home." "Okay," I said, knowing it would be impossible to wait.

I told her I was going to the coroner's office to pick up Rob's phone and keys, and then I was going to go to his apartment to see if there was a note or whatever the hell I might find.

I don't remember what either one of us said to end the call.

"One down, one to go," I said to Maura, who now looked as grief-stricken as anyone I've ever seen. I texted Zach to make sure he was around and then I made call number two.

"Yo yo," he cheerfully answered, like he always does.

"Yo, I have terrible news and there's no easy way to say it. Rob died. He killed himself," I said, rushing the words out as fast as I could.

Then I heard almost the exact same kind of crying that came from Caryn, only in a much deeper voice. And now I can describe it for you—it was the sound of our family being destroyed. I told him what I knew, we cried together, and then I suggested that he just go home.

There were no other words.

· *6* ·

We Are Extraordinary Parents

As long as we're on the subject of words, I find it strange that there's no word for a parent who loses a child. Why do widows, widowers, and orphans get to have all the fun? I think it's time for someone to right this wrong.

Bear with me for a moment as I reaffirm what you already know: children aren't supposed to die before their parents. That's just not the way life should work. We give birth to children or adopt them, we love and nurture them, we raise them, they grow up, we grow old, and then we die. The circle of life, sunrise, sunset, rinse and repeat, choose your own metaphor. That's what every parent expects, and by and large it's also the way things play out.

Losing a child—no matter the circumstances—goes against the natural order of things. It's not part of the ordinary experience. It is something entirely different, and we become something entirely different.

When your child is taken from you, you are no longer ordinary parents. Ordinary parents don't visit their child in a cemetery. Ordinary parents don't cry themselves to sleep at night. Ordinary parents don't wake up each morning knowing they'll never see their child again.

We become *extra* ordinary.

We become the ones who are unlike the others. We become the newest members of the world's cruelest club, one that is already over-crowded and where the cost to join is the steepest price imaginable. We become "those people," the tragic ones who are whispered about and pitied. We become the ones who are shattered, seemingly beyond repair. Remember Mary Tyler Moore in *Ordinary People*? That.

But after a while, something strange takes place that's right out of a Marvel comic book. A metamorphosis occurs during our grief and mourning, transforming us from extra ordinary to extraordinary. A lot happens when you close up the space between those two words.

We are extraordinary parents. Not in the sense that we are exceptionally good, which is what people usually mean when they use that adjective. But look it up and you'll find we are the very definition of the word:

> *a. Going beyond what is usual, regular, or customary b. Exceptional to a very marked extent*

We are extraordinary parents who must go on living in the world with a hole in our heart. We are extraordinary parents who, in many cases, still love and care for our other children. We are extraordinary parents who go to work every day and function as human beings, while most people are unaware of our secret identities. We are extraordinary parents who feel things that no ordinary parent has ever felt, and we can endure the deepest pain because that has become one of our superpowers.

And that's another notable thing about us: we all have different superpowers because each of us experiences our loss in our own particular way. Some of us have an unlimited capacity for compassion and forgiveness. Some of us become impervious to pain. Some of us are masters of disguise. Some of us can turn to stone. Some of us can become invisible. And then there are those of us who can open up and share it with the world.

We walk among you. We are your friends and neighbors, your co-workers, the quiet couple who sat at the table next to you in a restaurant last night. We are the extraordinary parents. And we don't mind if you want to call us by our first name.

One final word on words: many extraordinary parents, particularly in the early days of grief, feel like they're *broken*. I've always hated that self-appraisal. There's no doubt that we're damaged, but we are not broken.

Nothing calls for a good metaphor more than grief, and my favorite is *kintsukuroi*, the Japanese art of mending broken pottery by filling the cracks with gold or silver lacquer rather than trying to disguise the damage. The repair creates something even stronger and more beautiful than it was before.

Point being: that's exactly what happened to me and what can eventually happen to you.

• 7 •

Stuck in Suck City

$\mathcal{I}$'ve already talked about being gentle with yourself, and I'm sure you immediately took my recommendation and now you're feeling great. If only life worked that way! I wish there was some magic formula that could take away your pain and bring back your child, but there isn't and you, of course, knew that already. All the magic and wishes of the past are meaningless.

I can tell you that grief changes, time heals, and you'll get through this. That's all true, but none of it is happening now. Now, everything sucks and everybody sucks and the whole world sucks. So what are you supposed to do while you're stuck in Suck City?

Well, the first thing is simple: get out of bed. If you get out of bed in the morning, you've won. If you're able to take care of your other children, you've won. If you're able to get to work in one piece and function, you've won. If you're able to stop sobbing for a few minutes, you've won. What you've won won't be apparent for some time (here's a hint: it has to do with the realization that you have the tenacity to keep going), so for now just take the W and call it a day.

The second thing isn't as easy as the first, but it's not terribly difficult: do something creative—whatever that means to you—to express and channel your emotions. It will feel like a relief or a release or whatever it is you need to feel. And the best part is that you don't even need to know what you need to feel, because doing something creative— painting, drawing, journaling, dancing, gardening, you name it—has its own built-in rewards and surprises.

When Rob died, I started to write about him every day and never really stopped. It was the only way I knew how to grieve. I've written

27

about all of the most important things that have happened in my life and about all the people I love and have loved. Rob has always been right at the top of that list, as your children are surely on the top of yours.

When I wasn't writing about him, I was thinking about what I was going to write about him. It became an obsession, the only way I could cope with the excruciating emptiness of a world that kept turning without my son. Writing kept me connected to him, and I needed that more than anything. I needed it like I needed air. Every word I wrote was like taking a breath. It was like breathing life back into Rob.

What began as a labor of love, my way of trying to make sense of the unexplainable, eventually evolved into something much deeper, more meaningful, and universal, a creation that totally took me by surprise—namely, this book that you're reading right now.

The third thing is difficult, but if you're able to navigate the first two, I believe you owe it to yourself to take a whack at the third: face what scares you the most. Whatever that is. Be the hero in your own horror movie. Your grief is a scary beast, and it will hurt you and make you cry.

Grief hides in the shadows and creeps up on you when you least expect it, and when it does, here's the trick: don't fight it. The worse your pain gets and the deeper you can immerse yourself in it, the better and faster you'll move through it. Believe me, I know this is easier said than done.

There are no shortcuts, and you can't avoid grief for very long. I thought I could outsmart it or just go back to the early days of grief and deny it, but the scary beast is patient and lying in wait. Avoiding it just prolongs the whole process of healing. Like love, you can't hurry grief.

And it's perfectly okay to be afraid. We're all afraid of the unknown, of what comes next for us, of who we will become after we've endured the worst life has to offer. Grief asks more of us than anyone or anything has ever asked. The surprise of your life will come when you discover how much strength and courage has been hiding in your broken heart.

If this all sounds overwhelmingly daunting, it doesn't have to be. Like all large and imposing tasks, it's best to break it down into smaller, manageable pieces. For starters, think about what scares you the most. It's different for everyone. Maybe you're scared that as time passes, you'll forget your child's voice or the way he or she laughed. Or maybe you're scared that you'll never be happy again or that your family will never be the same. Or maybe you're scared of not being able to cope with the loss and that you'll remain miserable permanently. Or maybe you're deeply scared to return to the day your child died.

Whatever it is for you right now (and for certain that will change), look it in the eye every couple of days and stay with it for as long as you can. Dip a toe into the hot spring of your broken heart. Then do it again in the next few days and see if you can stand it for a few more seconds than you did the day before. You'll find it gets easier—never easy, but easier—and then one day, the scary grief beast will fade away like a distant childhood memory.

I know that life without your beloved son or daughter feels unbearable during the first few months after his or her death, but it won't always be like that. Suck City isn't where you live. It's just a place that you're visiting right now.

My time in Suck City actually began the day Rob arrived in Los Angeles, almost two years before he died.

I didn't want him to come to LA. I knew it would be a shit show because it was always a shitshow with Rob. I made up all kinds of excuses why he shouldn't come—he didn't have any money or a job or a place to live, and I told him that he couldn't stay with us in Venice because Maura worked from home, and we just didn't have the room. Mainly, I didn't want him moving here because of the drama that would inevitably come along for the ride, and the high anxiety and debilitating worry that I would suffer as a result.

So, of course, Rob headed west the next day. And Rob being Rob, he decided to travel across the country by train. The first act of the drama began after his train pulled out of Chicago. I got a frantic phone call from him saying that he needed to Venmo $750 to some dude he'd found on Craigslist who was going to hook him up with a share in an apartment in downtown LA. He said he didn't have a credit card and there was someone else interested in the place and he had to act fast. He swore he'd pay me back as soon as he arrived. The whole thing sounded sketchy, like many things Rob said and did, but I went ahead and "lent" him the money.

It was really happening. Rob was going to be living in LA.

The apartment sublet, unsurprisingly, turned out to be too good to be true. I'm not sure if it was a scam exactly, but apparently the management got wind of a bunch of illegal sublets and posted an eviction notice on their door. Rob had been in town for less than three weeks.

He said he might be able to find something with one of the other guys who was also being tossed, but that didn't pan out. After one night on the street, he called me early on a hot Saturday morning in June and said he had nowhere to live.

With me being me and Maura being the most loving and understanding person in the world and after crying to Caryn that I couldn't let him "bottom out" and live on the street, we decided that Rob would come live with us.

I drove downtown to pick him up and found him waiting outside the building wearing a pair of Chrome Hearts sunglasses that I had given him, the same style that David Duchovny wore in *Californication*. Rob had a few large boxes that were falling apart, overflowing with crumpled clothes, and a backpack almost as big as he was jammed with all kinds of stuff: more clothes, his high school yearbook, old concert ticket stubs, a few beer glasses with our last name etched on them, and his oddball collection of BIC lighters.

On the ride home, I told him that if he was going to live with us for a while there were two conditions: (1) He couldn't drink. (2) He had to go to AA. He was less than thrilled, particularly about the idea of attending daily meetings. I saw his face turn into "the other Rob," where the dark side lived. He did this weird thing with his jaw that looked like he was readying himself to take a punch, and his eyes got wide and angry before a kind of purple rage spewed out.

"I'm not going to fucking AA, Dad! You can stop the fucking car right here and I'll get out now," he said while we were driving in the middle lane on the 405 Freeway. "You can just leave me on the side of the fucking highway!"

"I can't stop here, Rob! And remember? You called me! I came to pick you up! These are the fucking rules!" I yelled back at him, banging the steering wheel with my fist.

We were both silent for the next twenty minutes.

"Okay, I'll go," he finally said in his softest voice while staring out the window.

· 8 ·

Handle with Care

*E*ver since Rob died, Zach and I say "I love you" every time we talk. In the past, we'd say it on each other's birthdays and when he was a little boy after tucking him in at night. He knows that I love him, and I know that he loves me, but there's something about actually saying the words that feels different to me now.

Despite how casually we may say them, those three little words carry a lot more weight than ever before. I feel them deeply, even after twenty minutes of us complaining about the Knicks and catching up on our favorite TV shows. I feel them in an urgent way that sometimes brings tears to my eyes, especially when I think about how thankful I am that we're both still alive to say them to each other.

On the other end of the spectrum, I didn't feel particularly thankful when I had to tell Zach that Rob had killed himself and when I was worried sick about how he was dealing—or not dealing—with it during the weeks and months that followed. It became a tricky balancing act, checking in with him regularly while trying to hold my own shit together, to say nothing of tending to Caryn and Maura's fraying emotions.

I rarely worried about Zach before, mainly because he rarely gave me anything to worry about. That was Rob's department. But when Rob died, Zach was suddenly promoted to department head.

I'd call him every couple of days to ask how he was doing while secretly probing for signs of trouble, which, as it turned out, existed only in my own troubled imagination. In fact, while writing this, I called him to help me remember exactly what we talked about during that dark period after Rob's death.

"I dunno, I remember reading whatever you had written about Rob on your blog that morning and we'd discuss it, and stuff like that," he recalled. "You suggested maybe talking to a shrink or joining a grief group a few times."

"Did I nag you about it? I sorta remember nagging you about it."

"Nah, you never nagged. We just talked the way we always do," he said. "Rob's death just became a part of our lives."

I couldn't have put it any better myself. I asked what else stood out during those grim early days without Rob.

"Hmm . . . I remember us talking about how every TV show we watched had a storyline about suicide," he said. "Like it was always in our face. Like we needed a reminder."

"It's true. I remember thinking, 'Should I warn Zach about one of the characters blowing his brains out or would that be too much of a spoiler?'"

"Haha! But it was really like in *everything*! Like it became the only way to die on TV."

"You know what that just reminded me of?" I asked.

"What?"

"Pretty much every time we talked, you asked how I was feeling. You were worried about me . . . like you didn't want me to die."

"I still don't!"

"Well, I don't either." We both cracked up. "It's funny how we can laugh about this now."

"I just remembered one more thing that really got on my nerves," Zach said.

"Tell me."

"The worst was when I heard my friends say, 'I had such a bad day at work I wanted to shoot myself.' Or they'd casually say, 'Kill me now' or 'I'm going to blow my brains out,'" he said with more than a tinge of annoyance in his voice. "They'd say these phrases without thinking and I had to tell them to be a little more aware of the words coming out of their stupid mouths. I know they didn't mean anything by it, but still."

We chatted for a few more minutes, said our I love yous, and hung up. There's nothing sweeter than seeing your little boy mature into a fine young man.

Beyond repeating those three little words as much as you can, the best approach to supporting your children who are grieving the death of a sibling is to do what comes naturally: check in with them as much as they'll allow, reassure them, gently offer advice if you think they may be open to it, listen without being judgy, and continue to love them with all of your being. In short, handle with care.

Because the truth is, there's nothing you can do or say that will help them heal. They'll need to do that for themselves. And they will—in their own time and in their own way—with your love and support. Their hearts are more resilient than ours because they're young and haven't had as much time to do serious damage to them.

And maybe try to steer them away from TV for a while.

· 9 ·

Terrible, Thanks for Asking

"So how ya doin'?"

I was never sure how to answer that question. Should I tell the truth, or should I tell whoever asked it what they wanted to hear?

One of the most difficult things among so many terribly difficult things about grief is that the person who grieves—the person in pain, particularly the person in the worst type of pain (and really, any pain is the worst kind of pain when it's your pain)—almost always has to wear a mask.

I'm not talking about when you're freshly bereaved and no one expects you to disguise your despair. During those first few days and weeks, you have no control of your emotions and you couldn't hide them even if you wanted to. Early on, people couldn't be kinder and more empathetic, not just your friends, but almost everyone you encounter. Total strangers are understanding and supportive. Early on, you see the very best in people.

Every book on grief stresses the importance of community and having a support system, and every book is right, but that community often comes with an expiration date. As time wears on, the griever (you) is still in severe pain but increasingly reluctant to dump his or her heartache on friends and loved ones. So we tend to shut up or, even worse, pretend we're getting along just fine. Cut to Dick Van Dyke singing, "Gray skies are gonna clear up, put on a happy face!"

And for the most part, your friends and relatives are more than happy to go along with this duplicity. They're relieved to hear this hopeful news because they love you and only want the best for you, and also because talking about depressing things is incredibly uncomfortable

35

and nobody is any good at it. It's easier to just talk about whatever you usually talk about—"Are you watching [fill in your favorite show]?" "Did you catch the [some team that you love] game?" "You must see the new [you get the idea] movie!" And let's just say that talking about your dead kid doesn't fall into any of these categories.

It's also important to note that our friends have, more or less, moved on from our tragedies, and rightfully so! That's just the way life works; everyone has their own stuff to contend with. Yet at the same time, they're also aware and respectful that we're still grieving. So we tacitly make a deal.

This is when we slip on our mask of normalcy and enter the world of make-believe. We say we're hanging in there. We say we're doing the best we can. We say that we're taking it one day at a time and that we're not crying as much as we used to. My go-to was "I'm not terrible," and that was on a good day.

So yes, I was hanging in there, but only by a thread. I was doing the best I could, but that didn't alleviate the sorrow. I was taking it one day at a time, but many of those days were a nightmare. I wasn't crying as much, but when I did it still hurt like a motherfucker. I was "not terrible," but I was miserable and had hardly any good days in the weeks and months after we lost Rob.

I had to wear an extra-special mask with Zach, Caryn, and Maura. The last thing I wanted to do was to make any of them feel worse than they already felt. Sure, we talked about Rob sometimes, but we mainly kept it on the surface because we knew the scary grief beast could pounce at any moment.

After some time (let's say months), the griever (that would be you again) really has no one to talk to about his or her loss (present company excluded). You can maybe get a few words in edgewise at grief group, and you could chat about it with your therapist for fifty minutes a week, and that's if you don't have any other more pressing problems to discuss, which seems crazy, but it's true, because life has to go on for us too.

This led me to the realization that we all must go through grief alone. It's a solitary act, like praying, the ultimate free solo. It's the dark night of the soul 24/7, especially during the early days, because grief never closes.

At the end of those days, when I took off my superhero mask and no longer felt particularly extraordinary, I just closed my eyes so I could be with my thoughts.

"So how ya doin'?" Rob would ask, in a little-boy voice from a long time ago.

"Just fine now," I'd reply.

Every Picture Tells a Story

$\mathcal{S}$ome parents find it too painful to look at old photos of their child. I felt the opposite. Going down memory lane and seeing photos of Rob as a kid and as an adult kept me connected to him, and that's what I needed the most in the first few months after his death.

If that's not what you need the most, I get it, but I'd still suggest looking at a photo or two every now and then. Viewing old photos is like time traveling. There's your child, growing up right before your eyes, until it stops before it's supposed to stop. It's heartbreaking, I know, and the anguish can be too much to bear, but if you can somehow stick with it, a bittersweet joy eventually arises from these photographic ashes.

At least that was the way it worked for me. I'd often start my tour at the top of the stairs with my all-time favorite photo—a framed poster-sized picture of me and the kids in our backyard when we lived in Long Island. It was taken for a story about having testicular cancer that I wrote for GQ more than twenty-five years ago. Zach's wearing an Allan Houston Knicks jersey and Rob's wearing a rare Michael Jordan Bulls jersey (45 was his number when he returned to Chicago after playing baseball). We're all barefoot, which I always thought was such a sweet touch. It's the most beautiful photo of the three of us ever taken, and looking at it made me sadder than any other photo in the house.

Hanging on another wall upstairs is a picture we called "The Menendez Brothers." It was also taken in our backyard, right around the time the real Menendez brothers were convicted of murdering their parents. Both kids (maybe they were three and four) wear black sweatshirts and sport identical "deer in the headlights" looks.

Downstairs on the first floor is the photo that accompanied the first *Esquire* story I wrote about Robbie. That's the one I look at—and talk to—most often, as it sits right across from our dining room table, where I'm routinely parked at my laptop. It's the only portrait that captures who Rob was on the inside, and that's why I took it out of storage after he died.

I used to have it hanging on a wall in my old apartment in Park Slope, Brooklyn. But then a feng shui expert came to my place and noted that none of the photos of my kids showed them smiling, something that had never occurred to me. I just thought the pictures were beautiful and kind of sophisticated.

Taking her advice to heart, I replaced them with "happier" snapshots, and those are the photos that came to sit on my bookcase in Los Angeles. On the top shelf is one of Rob and Zach, taken on Zach's eighteenth birthday. His presents included a skydiving jump and his first tattoo, and I remember all of us having such a great time that day.

Just below that photo is another all-time favorite, a shot of the two of them as teenagers. I must've somehow made them laugh, because their smiles are so big and genuine that you can feel how much they love each other. Zach prized this pic so much that he got a tattoo of it on his back several years before Rob died. We all used to joke about how the tattoo artist didn't do such a hot job in the likeness department, making both kids look—how should I put this?—mentally challenged. But Zach finally had another artist touch it up and now it looks exactly like the original photo.

On the next shelf is a shot of the kids taken by Caryn for my birthday. Rob is holding a sign that says, "Happy Birthday," and Zach's sign says, "Daddy We Love You." They must've been four or five and both are wearing party hats.

On the bottom shelf is another all-time fave, and I know I keep repeating that phrase but isn't that what we do? It's not like I'm going to hang photos of Rob having a meltdown at Disney World! This beauty shows my father-in-law, Marty, holding Rob's little hands while he's standing in Marty's lap. This is right around Rob's first birthday, and he's smiling at the camera while Marty is smiling hard at his grandson. It captures a moment of pure joy that, years later, has turned to irrevocable sadness because both of these two people I loved so dearly are no longer with us.

Yet there's something sweet about that sadness: a reminder of the depth of the connection that I felt—and continue to feel—with Rob.

• *11* •

The People in Your Heart
Will Make You Cry

I like to consider myself a world-class crier, but I wasn't always like that. One of the reasons I went into therapy many years ago was that I didn't shed a tear when my mom died. I thought I was just another regular guy, keeping my emotions bottled up like my father and his father before him, but the truth was that I was petrified to feel the excruciating pain of her loss. Hundreds of hours and thousands of dollars later, the floodgates finally opened and they've never fully closed.

I cried when I was happy. I cried when I was sad. I cried when I was scared. I cried when I was relieved. I cried when I was alone. I cried when I was with women. Indeed, women have always been able to make me cry, and once or twice it was even for joy.

One of the things I've learned over the years is that the people in your heart will make you cry—that's just the way the waterworks work.

But nothing approached the way I cried when Rob died.

It was a feeling I had never felt before and will never feel again. It was the feeling that I was scared to face when my mother died . . . only a million times worse. Rob cracked me wide open, and I sobbed and sobbed, pouring out what was left of my mangled heart.

I cried in Maura's arms when we first got the news. I cried the moment I saw Zach and Caryn when I flew into New York for the funeral. I cried when I saw Tony and Gina the night before we buried Rob. I cried when I saw my sister and her husband and every one of my friends who attended Rob's funeral and shiva.

I want to tell you that all my crying felt good, that it was a tremendous relief, but I don't remember anything like that. I just remember bursting into tears without a thought in my head. I was all feelings and none of them felt good.

Except that they were.

I didn't know it at the time, but I know it now. I know it because I saw the parents in my grief group weep for almost two years, and I witness other bereaved parents crying in grief groups that I now lead every week. I've seen how their tears have helped all of them to process their loss. I've seen how people slowly come back to life and transform into better versions of themselves, and it all starts with crying.

Crying is the primal soundtrack to the pain of missing your child, the heavy metal of our heavy hearts. It's uncontrollable, excruciating, overwhelming, and, above all, indispensable. You must hurt before you heal, and your tears will help repair your soul.

They did for me, and it all started the first night I joined a grief group. Someone had recently dropped out and I dropped in, an official member of the saddest club on the planet. As part of an exercise (and instead of doing what everyone was instructed to do), I asked if I could read something I had written about Rob. I chose a snarky obit, which I thought would be a shorthand way to introduce the group to my son and also because I thought it was funny, not yet understanding that there were not a lot of laughs in that group.

As soon as I began reading it aloud, I choked up.

Robbie Carlat, who could be a pain in the ass but was loved deeply by so many, died on Thursday morning in Long Beach, California. He was twenty-eight.

And there I was, bawling just like I did when I read Rob's eulogy at the funeral. At the time, I wasn't sure what triggered it, but in retrospect all the things we do to trick ourselves into not feeling the pain don't work in that room, where our defenses are down and we're all so raw and vulnerable. It's the one and only place to share how we're dealing with our loss where everybody knows exactly what you're talking about. And I think it may have also been about me hearing those terrible words out loud, which landed with a sickening finality that I hadn't anticipated.

That said, I still think it's a good way to tell you a little more about Rob, so here's the rest of the obit.

His father and spokesperson for the family, Larry Carlat, said the cause was "an unusually ridiculous level of stupidity."

Robbie Carlat was a restaurant manager for the past seven years, most recently serving as the food and beverage supervisor at Hustler Casino in Gardena,

California. Prior to that, he was the manager of Winston Pies in Brentwood. Mr. Carlat was also a competent chef, and his specialties—grilled burgers, Philly cheesesteaks, and Buffalo chicken wings—are fondly remembered in Venice Beach and Syosset culinary circles.

Known as "the king of shenanigans," Mr. Carlat, a bright, charming, and very funny young man, packed a lot of living into his twenty-eight years, though he harbored a darker side and was occasionally self-destructive, according to those who had shared a house with him. "He could be a real fuckin' idiot sometimes," said the family spokesperson.

Robbie James Carlat was born on January 18, 1991, in Joplin, Missouri. He was adopted at birth by Caryn and Larry Carlat. "It was love at first sight," said the family spokesperson, who spent much of the early days with the younger Mr. Carlat eating crap, yelling at him, and watching inappropriate movies. That pattern, known as "hanging with Rob," never fundamentally changed in their ensuing years together.

Mr. Carlat grew up in Woodbury, New York, and went to Walt Whitman Elementary School, Thompson Middle School, and Syosset High School. He briefly attended Farmingdale State College before moving to Binghamton, New York, where he sold weed to many of the stoner kids on campus at SUNY Binghamton.

"When Robbie moved in with me in Binghamton, I felt like I got to bring an important piece of home with me," said Jacob Silverman, a childhood friend who met Mr. Carlat in sixth grade.

Mr. Carlat had many girlfriends over the years but never married. He had no children—that we know of—though not for lack of trying.

"He'd go after any girl, not afraid of the possible rejection, and it was crazy because it worked the majority of the time. He was such a ladies' man," said his best friend, Sarah Miller.

Mr. Carlat was a rare combination, according to those who knew him intimately, of heartbreaker and heartbroken.

He is survived by his parents, Larry and Caryn, who declined to be interviewed for this article, his brother Zachary, who also declined to be interviewed but not before adding, "Dad, I don't feel like crying right now," and his cat Biscuit, whose whereabouts remain unknown.

• *12* •

Scream Real Loud

$\mathcal{S}$ometimes you just need to scream real loud.

• *13* •

The Twelve Steps of Grief

$\mathcal{W}$e're all familiar with the iconic Kübler-Ross five stages of dying and grief: denial, anger, bargaining, depression, and acceptance. What you may not be familiar with is the origin of the five-stage model, which was intended to anticipate the evolution of grief for people with a terminal diagnosis who are preparing for the end of life. In other words, it was never intended to be used *after* a death for the people who are left behind grieving, and it has since been widely and wildly misinterpreted.

Even by me, which you'll see when we return to these five fun fellows in the future. All I'll say about them now is that people experience these responses differently, at different times, and in no particular order—if they experience them at all.

Some of you may also be familiar with the twelve steps of recovery. I wasn't. I knew a little about it because of Rob, but I never took the time to learn what they're about. One thing that has stayed with me, however, is the Serenity Prayer, which is usually recited at the beginning of twelve-step meetings. I've never been a believer, but I found myself saying it often after Rob died.

> God, grant me the Serenity to accept the things I cannot change,
> Courage to change the things I can,
> and Wisdom to know the difference.

It took me a while to accept the thing I couldn't change (i.e., Rob killing himself), and the courage and wisdom parts will always be a work in progress. Although I'm not sure how I feel about the God part, it's

45

still a perfect prayer. So I thought if that invocation eased my suffering, taking a closer look at the twelve steps couldn't hurt.

The steps are uniquely designed to help people get sober and recover, but the principles behind each of them, which come straight from the AA "Big Book," are what really caught my attention. Being a writer, I started by looking at the key words associated with each of these principles:

Honesty
Hope
Faith
Courage
Integrity
Willingness
Humility
Love
Forgiveness
Acceptance
Awareness
Service

Some pretty good ones there, right? Like the Kübler-Ross stages, some of them may make sense to you now and some may make sense to you later. All I can tell you is how they made sense for me.

Love was what it was all about from the moment I saw Rob's beautiful face when he was born, to the end when he looked like he was peacefully asleep in his casket. I've never loved anyone the way I loved Rob and I never will.

Forgiveness followed. I forgave Rob for what he did because he was mentally ill, and I forgave myself for being unable to get a handle on his mental illness.

Faith burst out of me from a previously unknown place in my heart. I had a strong belief that I'd somehow find the *courage* and *willingness* to face the scary grief beast until he finally said adios.

Honesty, integrity, and *awareness* came naturally, not because I'm a saint—hardly!—but rather because, as I've said before, Rob's death cracked me wide open, and I've remained open and present in the moment ever since.

Humility is a given. Nothing humbles a person to their core more than the death of a child.

Acceptance is sort of everything rolled up into one big sad enchilada. Accepting the unacceptable meant facing the reality of never seeing Rob again and learning to live with it.

Service came as a huge surprise to me. I was never a "servicey" type of a guy, but after deciding that I wanted to help other parents like us, I found it truly was and continues to be one of the most rewarding things I've ever done in my life.

Hope is my second favorite word after love. Hope is everything. Hope keeps you going. Hope is what you need to get your arms around. Hope is what this book is all about.

Hope was what I held on to when Rob first came to live with Maura and me in Venice, and I insisted that he go to daily AA meetings. I wasn't sure what good they would do him, but I didn't think it would hurt and it gave me the illusion of control, which was the closest I would ever get to controlling Rob.

To show Rob that I meant business, I went with him to the first meeting in Santa Monica just a few hours after he had unpacked and made himself comfortable in our house. I drove to an address I had plugged into my GPS and pulled up to a church.

"I'm not sure we're allowed in there, Dad," Rob said dryly, sounding a whole lot like me.

"It's true. I don't know a lot of Jewish alcoholics," I joked back. "We're more a tribe of drug addicts and pill poppers."

A few middle-aged women smoking cigarettes outside nodded at us, and we nodded back like we were old pros. The truth was that neither of us felt thrilled to be there.

Apparently, there was some kind of pre-meeting private thing going on inside the church. They told us we could go in as soon as it was finished. We didn't have a clue about what to expect other than what we had seen in the movies and on television.

"You guys can go in now," said one of the smokers a few minutes later and so we did. Inside were fifty or so chairs arranged in a large semicircle, a few rows deep, with one chair in the middle. So of course

Rob and I made a beeline to the back where there were some scattered folding chairs. I sat down while Rob grabbed a cup of coffee. As I looked around, I noticed a few people talking to each other, but on the whole, it was like everywhere you go these days—most people were buried in their phones.

"This place is packed," Rob said as he sat down.

"I know! And I saw a bunch of beautiful women here," I said. "This place could be better for you than Tinder."

Rob just nodded and sipped his coffee.

The meeting began with what I came to learn is the AA Preamble. The one line I recall is: "The only requirement for membership is a desire to stop drinking." Then came the Serenity Prayer.

"Here we go with the fuckin' God shit," Rob whispered to me. "I like that you're keeping an open mind," I whispered back.

A woman in the center of the semicircle who was running the show asked if there were any newcomers at the meeting who would like to introduce themselves. A few people raised their hands. We were not among them.

"Raise your hand!" I mouthed to Rob. "You raise your fuckin' hand," he mouthed back.

Then it was time for the "Hello, my name is . . . " and "I'm an alcoholic" sharing stuff. There were multiple mentions of the "Big Book," but beyond that, I don't remember much about what was said or anyone in particular, other than one intense dude who was covered in tats and reminded me of the famous tough guy Chuck Zito.

That was followed by a few announcements about a picnic and who was assigned to bring what and something about getting court vouchers signed before leaving. Then I noticed people passing a basket. When it got to me, I threw in a five to cover the two of us.

At the end of the meeting, everyone in the room stood up and held hands while reciting the Lord's Prayer. I held Rob's hand tight, feeling cautiously optimistic. A number of people who shared stories that day had gone through way worse hell than Rob had, and now they were in recovery, living their lives, as the saying goes, one day at a time.

After the big "Amen," a few folks milled around while some other guys started to stack the chairs. Rob surprised me by helping them out, and then we split. The steps for walking the straight and narrow were there, if only Rob would take them.

"So other than the God stuff, what did you think?" I asked as we walked back to the car.

"It was all right," Rob said, lighting a cigarette. "I liked the tattoo guy."

"I thought it was really interesting," I said, perhaps a little too enthusiastically.

"Well, good for you," Rob said.

· 14 ·

Reality Bites

$\mathcal{O}$n a sweltering summer day many years ago, Caryn and I took the kids to Sesame Place, a water theme park outside of Philadelphia. I remember going on a Big Bird water slide with Zach, who was still in diapers, and we had to wait in a long, snaking line as we made our way to the top of the slide.

We were both super excited when we finally got there, and Zach was squeezing my hand tight. There were a few big kids in front of us who were jostling each other, and then all of a sudden, I didn't feel Zach's hand anymore. When I looked down, he was gone.

I immediately started to panic. He was nowhere in sight and a sickening feeling enveloped me. I remember thinking—just for a split second—what if someone snatched him and I've lost him forever, and *oh my god, oh my god, oh my god, Zach!* My heart was beating wildly until I saw him sitting down, just a few feet away, behind one of the big kids. The whole thing couldn't have lasted more than a minute, but it felt like a lifetime—specifically, Zach's. This Big Bird trauma left its mark on me, returning, with a vengeance, the day Rob died.

I know you know that feeling. You also know that you don't lose someone once, you lose them every day. Some mornings when you wake up, it all feels like a terrible dream. Like it never happened. That's when it's the worst. I remember thinking, *How can Rob be dead?* Like he was Andy Kaufman pulling an elaborate prank.

The whole thing is surreal, there's no sense of time, and nothing makes sense. When you lose a child, your world is suddenly incomprehensible. You're in an altered state, adrift in uncharted waters. You are crushed, numb, and in shock. You're in a fog of stunned disbelief.

51

Then, little by little, the fog lifts, and everything becomes very clear, very sharp, very painful, and very real—your child is dead. That's it. End of story. Reality bites.

Accepting the reality of your loss is one of grief's greatest hits and those hits keep coming. Of course, your head knows that your child is gone, but your heart has to endure the pain of all that hitting. If there's any good news to be found here, it's this: whenever you feel the pain and whatever triggered it is an inescapable reminder that you're very much living in the real world and managing your grief as best you can.

There was nothing more painfully real than seeing Rob's death documented on paper. I was especially bummed out the day his death certificate arrived. It made the whole thing feel so permanent. It was way easier to get lost in melancholy memories and photos of Rob rather than being confronted with the stark finality of it all. I remember thinking, "Are we supposed to hang this thing up on a wall like it's some sort of diploma? Like we're now graduates of the university for parents who have lost a child?" I'd hate to see that sticker on the back of a car window.

It was a very official-looking document with old-timey blue squiggles bordering the edges that was supposed to make you feel all serious, this means business, we're not fooling around here. It contained all the relevant details—name, date of birth, date and time of death, occupation, and address.

Underneath that info is where we came in. First, there was something called "Informant," with my name typed in all caps followed by a comma and the word "Father." Caryn and I were listed under "Parents."

Then came reliving the fun part—place and cause of death. It was like playing a game of Clue: *it was Colonel Mustard in the study with a revolver.* Rob wouldn't have taken kindly to being Colonel Mustard and would never be caught dead in the study, which sounds too much like being in school.

There was some other bits and pieces about the funeral establishment and where he's buried, and on the line devoted to "Manner of Death" an *X* appeared in a tiny box next to the word "Suicide." This may be obvious, but I'll say it anyway: there's not a whole lot of life in death certificates.

The police report arrived a few weeks later. I had hoped that I'd find something new that would somehow reveal the mysteries behind Rob's disappearing act, but this report was just a lot of what I already knew and a bunch of miscellaneous details that dredged up disturbing questions.

The first page, "Administrative Information," was just the facts, ma'am—name, race, sex, address, that kind of thing. The next three pages were "Narrative," which began with dispatch receiving a call about a shot fired and then another one reporting a suicide attempt: "CP says friend shot himself." CP stands for "calling party."

That was followed by the names of the responding officers and a detailed description of the location, complete with compass-like directions ("The kitchen was north of the living room, the bedroom was south of the living room"). Under the heading "Upon Arrival," the report said the CP and another witness were on the fifth floor pointing the police to the sixth floor, where Rob lived. The police knocked on his door, announced themselves, and then entered the apartment. The decedent—that's Rob—was lying on the floor with an apparent gunshot wound to the head.

The Long Beach Fire Department and Rescue arrived on the scene next, and a paramedic pronounced Rob dead at 2310 hours (that's ten after eleven to us civilians). One of the witnesses stated that the body wasn't moved after the gunshot and that the decedent had a history of alcohol abuse. Rob was identified as being in his early to mid-twenties, 120 to 140 pounds, and there was a list of his tattoos. It went on to describe the placement of his body, again with GPS precision: "His legs were facing south. His elbows were pointing east and west." The report then noted what Rob was wearing: gray long-sleeve sweatshirt, black belt, blue jeans, black socks, and brown shoes. White Apple earbuds were protruding from underneath the sweatshirt.

A black revolver was found on the floor next to his left foot. There was a pool of blood near his head and spatter by his feet. A bullet fragment was located on the floor in the living room, and black eyeglasses were found in the northeast corner of the kitchen. The report added: "It should be noted, there were several empty 25-ounce cans of Hurricane malt liquor scattered throughout the apartment."

An investigator from the Coroner's Office arrived on the scene. She took photos, recovered a .38 Special cartridge, gathered Rob's iPhone and keys to the apartment, and then took possession of the body.

There was a bunch of other minor details on page 4 about follow-up reports, a canvassing of the surrounding apartments (known as "knock and talks"), and how another officer took custody of Rob's cat and transported it to Long Beach Animal Shelter. And that was pretty much all she wrote. Thanks for nothing, Long Beach Police Department.

Last but not least came the Grim Reaper's Report. I gotta give the coroner's office credit, this one was far and away the most comprehensive, weighing in at a hefty thirteen pages. It even included stock illustrations of a body with annotations indicating everything from Rob's tattoos to the gunshot entry and exit wounds.

There really wasn't very much new info in it, but the report did contain a few interesting tidbits, beginning with the fact that no drugs were detected, according to the laboratory analysis, just high levels of alcohol. They had Rob's weight at 117 pounds, which, strangely, made me tear up. The phrase "gunshot wound of the head" appeared no less than five times in the first few pages.

After reading these piece-of-shit reports again and again, I was still at a loss—good phrase there—desperate to connect the dots. So many questions continued to swirl around in my head, and I tortured myself with endless theories and scenarios of who did what to whom, but I knew that it wouldn't make a difference. Nothing could bring Rob back.

· 15 ·

Everything Is Going to Be Okay

$\mathscr{I}$ need to repeat this sentiment throughout this book because I feel it profoundly and I need you to feel it too—everything is going to be okay. It's so difficult to see and feel that right now, but the fog will lift, the pain will diminish, and you will make it through to the other side of the rest of your life.

It's amazing that we can go on without a part of us. It's like the "phantom limb" syndrome, when people who have lost an arm or a leg continue to feel that their lost limbs are still attached. That's the way I feel about Rob. I'm still very much attached.

And yet in many ways I have let go. I've let go of denial. I've let go of guilt. I've let go of anger. I've let go of fear. I've let go of sadness. Maybe that's why the grief beast became less scary and pretty much let go of me. The worst thing in the world has happened, the dust has settled, and I'm still standing in the rubble with the spirit of Rob by my side.

You are still standing, too, and you will ultimately find your way through. How you get there will be different from how I got there and how others get there, but once you get there, you'll find that you're not the same person that you were before. We'll never be the same, just like we were never the same after our child was born. Grief reshapes you into a better version of yourself. That's how we transform from ordinary to extraordinary parents. It's impossible to see yourself in that light now, but after you've finished this book and have begun to heal, I feel certain that you will.

It will take time—and patience—because we are all on our own personal grief clock. It took me about two years to make a kind of peace with losing Rob, and it will take you however long it takes you. Grief is cyclical. It often feels like you're stuck in an endless loop, telling yourself the same stories over and over again (just as you'll notice certain recurring themes, suggestions, and reminders echoed in the chapters to come). Grief lasts until the day we die and so does our love for our lost child. The heartache becomes a part of us that we incorporate into our lives.

It's hard work, and you'll have to make two important decisions along the way, which is no easy task when you're in such a fragile state and your grief prevents you from seeing straight. The first begins with a question: are you willing to face your pain and move through it to get to the other side? If your answer is yes, the second decision comes a little further down the grief road when you recognize that you can *choose* how to move forward, reengaging with the world, taking better care of yourself, and enjoying your life.

I remember having this epiphany right after the first anniversary of Rob's death, thinking that's what he would want me to do. I was looking at a photo of his smiling face, and I somehow interpreted it as a ray of hope. Hope is the light at the end of the grief tunnel. It may be just a flicker now, but it will shine brightly again.

You will laugh again. Food will taste delicious again. Music will sound wonderful again. You will find joy again. It will feel good to be alive again. You'll cherish and be grateful for the time you have left because you've learned that every day is a precious gift.

That's what I was thinking just the other day when I was walking on the beach, listening to Kanye West's "24," a gospel-tinged tune dedicated to Kobe Bryant that always tugs at my heart. I took a moment to look at the sky and saw a large cloud formation that resembled a giant smiling rabbit. There's a refrain in the song where Kanye and a choir sing, "We gonna be okay," over and over again, and I started to sing along, and—I realize how incredibly corny this sounds—that's when I imagined the rabbit in the sky was Rob smiling down on me.

So, corny or not, I'll repeat it one more time—we gonna be okay.

• 16 •

Me and You

$\mathscr{I}$ thought it might be helpful to check in with each other at the end of each part of this book, so let's do it.

> ME: I'll start by asking what everyone has been asking you: how are you doing?
>
> YOU: I'm okay today. Yesterday wasn't the best and tomorrow, I have no idea! I've been trying to be gentle with myself, but it's difficult.
>
> ME: Grieving the death of your child is the hardest thing you'll ever do. Being gentle with yourself just cuts down on the self-inflicted wounds.
>
> YOU: I've been feeling overwhelmed. It's not one thing; it's everything that's happening and not happening.
>
> ME: What do you mean?
>
> YOU: Like you said, there are no words. I have such a hard time talking about it. I don't know, I just thought grief was going to get easier. Isn't that the way it's supposed to work? Time heals and blah blah blah?
>
> ME: Well, it really hasn't been a lot of time. And I hate to break it to you, but grief lasts a lifetime.
>
> YOU: So I've heard. Maybe I just thought there would be less pain by now. I'm still so incredibly sad most of the time. I'm not even sure if this is grief or mourning. What's the difference?
>
> ME: Grief is what you think and feel when someone you love dies. Mourning is more about dealing with the loss. In other words, grief

is the beginning of mourning. Are you doing anything for yourself that makes you feel any better?

YOU: Not really a whole lot other than getting together with friends. They're all such good listeners and I'm grateful to have them in my life.

ME: Well, I'm glad to hear that. What do you guys talk about?

YOU: Mainly how I'm feeling or not feeling. I've tried to share stories and I've tried to look at photos, but after a few seconds, I lose it and start sobbing uncontrollably.

ME: As weird as it sounds, crying is a good thing.

YOU: It doesn't feel good. Nothing feels good.

ME: Anything and everything you're feeling right now is perfectly okay to feel. There's no right way or wrong way to grieve. Grief isn't a problem to be solved. It's a process to be lived.

YOU: I wouldn't call whatever it is I'm doing "living."

ME: You are a parent who has recently lost a child and you're hanging in there. Maybe cut yourself a little slack.

YOU: Well, I'm not feeling particularly extraordinary at the moment, if that's what you mean.

ME: You'll get there. There's a lot more road to travel.

YOU: That's what scares me. That the road will never end. That I'll always have this gaping hole in my heart.

ME: Grief will be a part of you, as well as who you become, but the pain will lessen with time. It will never completely go away because your child lives on in your heart.

YOU: Sure, okay, but you can't have lunch with your heart. You can't give your heart a hug or put your arm around his shoulders. I keep asking *why*. Why am I still here when my child is gone? Why did this happen to him? Why did this happen to me? Why should I go on living?

ME: All the "whys" in the world can't bring your child back. I know you know that. What hurts the most right now?

YOU: I don't even know where to start. I'm depressed, cranky, and then I'm filled with rage, and then I'm confused and frightened.

Sometimes I feel guilty and other times I can't feel anything. Worst of all is when I think about my child not being here and how I'll never see him again. When I get stuck in that dark, dark place, it sends a shiver of terror down my spine and across my chest until I feel a nauseating emptiness bubbling up somewhere in my throat.

ME: Sounds to me like you're feeling exactly what you should be feeling.

YOU: Um . . . er . . . thanks? I wouldn't wish this on anyone. The pain is unbearable and then there's the agony of seeing my other children suffer. Hearing them sob is excruciating, and I feel completely helpless because there's nothing I can say or do to console them.

ME: All you can do is be there for them. You can't take away their pain. Listen to them, hug them, support them. Just love them the way you've always loved them.

YOU: I loved my lost child more than anything in the world and . . .

ME: . . . and it wasn't enough. It was the same for me.

YOU: I keep thinking about what would have happened if I had done things differently. What if I was a better parent? What if I was tougher or more understanding? What if I was more controlling . . . or less controlling? What if I held on instead of letting go? What if I let go instead of holding on as tight as I held on? And then I think, what if I never had children in the first place?

ME: All those what-ifs like to tag along with the whys. You can talk about them from now 'til doomsday, but doomsday, as you well know, has come and gone. Now you're left with processing your grief, which really means looking at it and moving through it. I keep repeating these things because I feel it's important for you to keep hearing them.

YOU: I appreciate it. I just miss him so much, and it hurts so much to look at that grief, much less move through it. Sometimes I just feel like I've been emptied out and there's nothing left of me. And you know what's the worst?

ME: Tell me.

YOU: The worst is being pitied. I hate that! I don't want to be that person. I don't want people feeling bad for me behind my back. And in front of my back is just as confusing because I'm never sure how people really feel about me. Are they just being kind because my kid has died?

ME: You can't control what other people say or think. All you can do is take good care of yourself. I know it hurts, and I know it hurts even more when you force yourself to really look at your loss, to really feel it in your heart of hearts.

YOU: Sometimes when I try to do that, I can't feel anything. I just feel numb. And that scares me too. I just feel . . . I don't know what I feel anymore. It keeps changing.

ME: It's going to take time to process the loss, and it's going to take time to build yourself back up into something that resembles a human being again, and it's going to take time for you to pick up all the pieces and transform into an extraordinary parent. That's the journey—that's where you are headed—and you will get there, and you will live a meaningful life again, perhaps even more meaningful than ever before.

YOU: I want to believe you. I really, really do. And now you've got me crying again. Can you give me a moment please?

ME: Take as much time as you need.

YOU: You keep saying that.

ME: Well, that's kinda how it works.

YOU: I'm beginning to get the picture. Sometimes I close my eyes and make up my own pictures. Like, I'll think how I'd give anything to have one more day with him, and then I'll think about us just being together like he is in my dreams.

ME: I think that, too, and I also see Rob in my dreams, and for whatever reason, he always comes to me as a child.

YOU: Goddamn it! I'm crying again. When will it stop hurting so much?

ME: I remember shortly after Rob died, I read something that I didn't really grasp back then, and you probably can't grasp right now, but I'm going to tell it to you anyway. Here goes: in order to get from *what was* to *what will be*, you must go through *what is*.

YOU: Sounds a little Yoda-ish to me. And you're right, I have no idea what you're talking about.

ME: That's okay. We just finished the end of *the end* and now it's time to take a look at and move through *the middle*.

Part II

THE MIDDLE

• 17 •

One Step Forward

*Y*esterday was okay. The day before, not so much. A few days before that? Sheer agony, taking you right back to the terrible day your child died. Tomorrow? Who knows? That's the way grief works. One step forward, two steps back.

There's no rhyme or reason. Every day is the opposite of a choose-your-own-adventure children's book. It feels like a new adventure is choosing *you*. That will change with time, but for now, you're just along for the ride. The ride goes round and round, backward and sideways, and does loop the loops. It kicks your ass and makes you crazy as you hang on to . . . you're not even sure *what* you're hanging on to anymore.

The ride takes you to places where you've never been before, places that scare the shit out of you, places that crack you wide open—all places we explore together in this middle part of the book.

But every now and then, the ride slows down for just a moment and you're able to catch your breath and, almost imperceptibly and mostly unintentionally, take one step forward.

It doesn't matter how small or fleeting it was. That one step—whatever it is for you—is huge. It means there's something stirring inside you. It means you're not stuck. It means you're heading in the right direction, even though you feel completely disoriented. There's no telling when or how you'll arrive at where you're going, but you'll know it when you get there.

If all this sounds cryptic, it's because it is. It's impossible to get your bearings when you're staggering around in the dark. And unfortunately, the forecast for the foreseeable future remains pretty much the same—pitch dark and heavy precipitation in most areas. You don't need a weatherman to tell you that. You know it better than anyone.

But what you don't know and can't see right now is the light. You're trapped inside the awful grief tunnel, but each step forward brings you closer to the shining light at the other end.

Most times, but not always, it's just a glimmer at first—a memory from long ago that brings a half smile to your face, a song on the radio that makes you well up, an insight gleaned from a TV character who reminds you of your kid—but it's important to recognize these small sparks of life, to really take them in and feel them in your bones.

Because the glimmers will intensify and become more frequent, eventually turning into sunbeams, and the baby steps will grow into purposeful strides, and one day you'll stop crying, and then the next day, you'll laugh more easily, and one step forward will become two steps, and then three, and all of a sudden, you're not going backward anymore, you're embracing life like your life depends on it (it does!).

You're stronger than you've ever been because you've endured the worst pain imaginable, and that tragedy has become a vital part of you—forever changed—maybe even for the better. That ineffable something to hang on to turns out to be *you*, bathing in the warmth of the shining light.

And then you'll discover that the most extraordinary thing has taken place while you didn't notice—your heart is no longer vacant. In fact, it's filled with love again, just like it was when your child was born. This is where their beautiful souls continue to live on, just like Rob lives on in mine. It doesn't make me miss him any less, but it's comforting to know that he's nearby, just where I need him.

But before any of that can happen, there are thousands and thousands of steps ahead of you.

• 18 •

A Swift Kick in the Ass

*M*y first step forward was a giant one, something that I already knew but had not accepted—Rob was mentally ill. Instead of a glimmer, this acknowledgment struck me like a thunderbolt about a month after he died, and it was the skeleton key I often used whenever I felt locked in my grief.

You wouldn't know it if you met him. He was smart, engaging, cool, and super funny. Over the years, he learned how to disguise his troubled mind and showed us what he thought we wanted to see.

He was first diagnosed with bipolar disorder when he was seventeen, and one of his therapists told us at the time that he was also an alcoholic. We knew Rob smoked and sold weed and dabbled in other drugs (no big deal—back in the day, so did I), but I distinctly remember thinking the shrink was crazy, because that's what I always did when it came to Rob. I chose to see what I wanted to see. I always chose to view him in the most hopeful and positive light even when everything he said and did pointed elsewhere. It was an act of self-deception that lasted until we lost him forever.

We always used euphemisms when we described Rob—difficult, impulsive, reckless, unpredictable, irrational—but we all knew the truth. Although I'm not sure he did. Sometimes he'd say he was having a bad day or wasn't feeling good, but that was the extent of it. Whether it was shame, denial, or a lack of self-awareness, Rob never fully acknowledged that he had a mental illness. He admitted that he was an alcoholic the day I drove him to his first sober house. And he texted Caryn two days before he died to say that he was seriously depressed and needed meds.

The only other times we ever talked honestly about what was raging inside his head was when he was in crisis and were forced to. The first instance happened when he was a senior in high school, and we had sent him to a mental hospital in Westchester for a month. A few Thanksgivings before he died, I drove him to the emergency room in Santa Monica after he threatened to kill himself. They put him on different medications each time, and each time he stopped taking them shortly thereafter.

When we first talked about dealing with the disease, walking on familiar eggshells, he was defensive and belligerent. When we talked about it ten years later in a psychiatric hospital, he was more compliant because he just wanted to get the hell out of there. There wasn't a whole lot of talk about it otherwise.

And once he moved to LA, it was really just about us being together. I never thought, *Oh, I'm just chillin' with my mentally ill, alcoholic son.* Sure, I knew the disease was there. A lot of times, I chose to ignore it or gently navigate my way around it, and a lot of times Rob chose to hide it, but for the most part, it was just us genuinely enjoying each other's company. In the last two years of his life, I saw Rob at his best and at his worst.

After he moved out of our place in Venice, I insisted on visiting him every Saturday afternoon in Torrance when he was living in a sober house because I needed to see him with my own eyes. I needed to see what he looked like and how he was acting (in both senses of that word) and it was generally just my way to tamp down my own endless worry and anxiety. I was also on the lookout for any clues that he had fallen off the wagon and possibly gone off the deep end again.

Mental illness isn't always obvious, even when it's staring you in the face. Even when it's talking to you and saying crazy things, it's easy to make excuses and rationalize what you see and hear. And that's what I did while he was out here, because it was easier, because it kept the peace between us, because it kept him close to me.

I remember telling one of my many therapists, a few months before Rob died, that I wished I had the guts to be straight with him and say the following:

> You need to go to a doctor and get meds for being bipolar. You need to get it under control. If you look back at when you've had horrible shit happen to you, it's always between October and December, and

that's when you get manic, and you need to do something about that or it's never going to change. You also need to take antidepressants. I've been there, dude, I know how it feels, and meds help! Go get fuckin' help! Go get fuckin' help before something terrible happens!

I didn't say any of that to him when he was alive, and it's one of the few things that will haunt me for all time, even though I'm aware that it wouldn't necessarily have done any good or changed the way things played out.

So my first step forward was a swift kick in the ass, understanding what Rob was struggling with and that I couldn't do anything to save him. I've taken many other steps since then, but none was as significant as that one great leap.

· 19 ·

Finding Your People

Joining a grief group was my second great leap forward. Other than playing sports and going to a few AA meetings with Rob, I had never done much of anything in a group. I've always tended to be a lone wolf rather than traveling in a pack. But I was in so much pain and knew from many years of therapy that I desperately needed to do something to help myself. So I googled "grief support," found Our House, and after an initial intake meeting . . . was put on a waiting list.

Although you wouldn't know it by the surface, grief is apparently very popular in LA.

I've told you about my first time at a grief group, which was about three months after that initial call to Our House. Now I'm going to tell you about yours.

The first thing you notice is everyone's eyes. It's the same look you see in the mirror every day. It's the vacant, thousand-yard stare, the look of someone who is not there. And that's the thing: you're all sitting shoulder to shoulder in a circle and, at the same time, you're all, to varying degrees, detached from reality.

The two group leaders ask you to briefly introduce yourself with your name, the name of your child, and how he, she, or they died. Then, one by one, that's what each member of the group does. You hear one horror story after another—overdoses, suicides, cancers, freak accidents, murders. It's absolutely brutal, and everyone is sobbing. You think, *Why am I subjecting myself to this misery-loves-company ordeal? How is this going to help me?* It takes everything in you not to get up and bolt.

You're then asked to tell your story in more detail, and after a few moments, you notice that everyone is nodding their heads in tacit acknowledgment, and you can feel that they know exactly what you're talking about. *Broken hearts*, you think, *recognize broken hearts.* And that realization comes as such a relief, like you had been holding your breath all of this time and can finally let it all out.

Here you are with other parents who understand what you've been going through, and sharing your trauma instantly connects you to them. (This phenomenon is known as "collective resonance" if you ever want to impress a roomful of therapists and mental health clinicians.) You're no longer alone. You're with your people.

There's a surprising power in being part of a group. Revealing your innermost thoughts and feelings—no matter how crazy you might think they are—to imperfect strangers who truly understand because they're pretty much feeling the same way, opens you up like nothing else. Once you realize that this is a safe place, perhaps the *only* place, where you can bare your darkest and most intimate thoughts, an unshakable trust is established. No one's judging you here, with the possible exception of yourself.

You look around the circle of sadness and see all kinds of people whom you would ordinarily never be friends with in the real world, but, as you now know, you no longer live in the real world. You're all trying your best to survive, to just get through one lousy day after another, and these people you've never met before are supporting you and hanging on to your every word. This moves you to tears again, and you think maybe you'll come back for a second meeting.

You decide to return (good call!), and every other week for the next two years you're sharing memories of your child or expressing your anger, guilt, frustration, sorrow, disbelief, longing—whatever it is you're struggling with or stuck on. You're also listening and processing, especially during the prolonged silences before and after each question, when your emotions tend to stew in their own juices. You still basically feel like crap, but now you have some fellow travelers along for the ride.

After a while, a truly profound thing begins to happen. You're about nine or ten months into your group when you first notice a shift. There are now occasional jokes and laughter in your meetings, maybe for the first time. Don't get me wrong, there's still plenty of crying. When your child dies, a darkness descends that feels like you're living in one of those Norwegian towns that doesn't see the sun for months on end. But all of a sudden, a ray of sunlight has entered the room. You think maybe it's the arrival of hope.

These total strangers, who have become your friends, are beginning to transform. It sort of sneaks up on you, but when you witness it in others, when you see a tiny spark in their eyes, when you see people coming back to life, well . . . it can take your breath away.

One of my favorite grief group memories took place before each of our meetings when I'd meet my friend Vic at a Chinese restaurant just a few blocks away from Our House. We were the only two single fathers in the group, and we shared stories about our lost sons while sharing copious amounts of food—including my beloved soup dumplings, in honor of Rob. Both of our boys were adopted and suffered from addiction issues. They were the same age when they died. Vic and I are basically two peas in a pod, which we never ordered because neither of us likes vegetables.

When we were done, we'd split the check, hop in our cars, and drive to our meeting. There was usually a bowl of candy sitting on the coffee table in our meeting room, and for dessert, we'd each take a Hershey's chocolate Kiss (or three), which always seemed to make talking about our boys a tiny bit sweeter.

Talk Therapy

$\mathcal{I}$ like to talk to Rob as if he were still here. Maybe you do the same with your child. I tell him how I'm doing and ask him about his day—or whatever measurement of time they use wherever he's hanging out. I tell him how Zach and his mom are getting along. I tell him about the shows I'm watching, especially the ones I think he'd like the most. I talk to him while I'm writing, and sometimes if I come up with a particularly eloquent line, I thank him for the inspiration.

"That was really nice, dude," I'll say out loud. "Keep up the good work!"

I know he can hear me and that he's watching over me. I often feel his presence or at least recognize a sign that he's dropped by for a visit. How do I know this? How do I know that all the things I hear him say aren't just the product of my overheated imagination—the Robbie movie endlessly playing in my head?

All I can tell you is this: I just know.

I just know because that's what I choose to believe. I believe Rob and I are having a conversation over my morning coffee or that he's helping me write this sentence right now ("Damn straight I am!" he just said and smiled). It feels good to believe. It brings me a measure of comfort and keeps me connected with him. As previously mentioned, Rob lives deep inside of my heart. He always has and always will.

As a matter of fact, I feel our relationship is better today than it was when he was alive. I know that sounds strange, but it really isn't. When Rob was with us, he could be a holy terror and he made me crazy with worry. I had a small heart attack every time the phone rang.

I don't anymore. We're all good now because I know he's all good now. I know Rob's at peace, basking in the sunlight.

It's his beautiful spirit—the essence of who he was—that I communicate with today. He can still be a sarcastic bastard, but that was one of the things I loved about him most. Rob will always be my son and I will always be his dad, whether he's here or not. I just heard him say "Damn straight!" again and felt a slight flutter in my chest.

Maybe you were lucky enough to have had a good relationship with your son or daughter and maybe they were destined to do great things. You miss them so bad and so intensely that you can't bring yourself to talk to them, much less hear their voice, because the pain of their absence is too much to bear. The idea that all of your child's hopes, dreams, and ambitions have been savagely dashed is excruciating to process, much less to accept.

I get it, I really do, but I recommend that you try to push through and talk to them anyway. It doesn't matter if they can hear you. It doesn't matter if they respond. What matters is expressing your love for your child. You loved them in life, you love them in death, you love them until the end of time. You need to tell them that. Every day. Tell them, tell them, tell them!

They are a part of you and will always be a part of you, and if you're open to it, you can learn a lot by listening to them. Just because they're dead doesn't mean they no longer have important things to tell you.

They will help shape you into the different person you're becoming. Your convos with them—as imagined as they may seem—are one of the best ways to process your loss. Talking to your child will tell you everything you need to know.

You'll always get a straight answer to any question.

I've asked Rob if there was anything I could've done to keep him here with us, and he told me that he tried, that he really tried, but he just couldn't deal with his inner sadness anymore.

Let them know how you're feeling.

A few months after Rob died, I was going on about how much I loved him and how I always thought that that would be enough, that the enormity of my love would always keep him safe, and how I felt like I somehow let him down. He surprised me by saying that was ridiculous and he felt that he had let *me* down.

They enjoy nothing more than a good joke.

Every time the Powerball payout reaches a billion or so dollars, I playfully ask Rob if maybe he could slip me the winning numbers. He says that giving out that type of information is frowned upon, but if he could, he'd give the lucky digits to his mom because he always liked her better. "You're still such a dumbass," I say to him. "Takes one to know one," he shoots right back.

Tell them how much you miss them.

Your child will hold your hand while drying your tears and reassure you that everything is going to be okay because they love you and only want you to be happy again and enjoy the rest of your life. They want that more than anything.

Rob told me so.

• *21* •

When Love Isn't Enough

*T*hanks mainly to the Beatles, I always thought that love was all you need. Love was the answer, I knew that for sure. As I've said many times and will continue to say, I've never loved anyone the way I loved Rob and I never will.

I'm sure you feel the same way about your child. That's the deal when you become a parent—the amount of unconditional love you feel for your children is so enormous and overwhelming that you didn't and couldn't possibly have known that you had it in you to give. There's a transformation that happens at your core when you become responsible for this tiny, new human being who is 100 percent dependent on you. The world shifts from revolving around yourself to revolving around your child. Your child becomes your world.

But when your world ends, as it has for so many of us, you learn a terrible truth about love, one that the Beatles never sang about. It's simply this: *love isn't enough to save the person you love.*

That insight has become something of a mantra for me. I can't get it out of my head because for the longest time, I thought it was. I thought love would be enough until Rob, the person I loved, made it very clear it wasn't.

I thought love would be enough when we first adopted him. I thought love would be enough when he cried incessantly and insisted I pick him up. I thought love would be enough when we had to deal with every scary thing that ever happened to Rob. Because, no matter what, we loved him with all of our hearts, even when he was at his most unlovable.

Admittedly, I was often blinded by that love. It was so strong, so immense, so all-encompassing that I believed it could do anything. Saving Rob was not only my job as his father, it was my superpower. I can't tell you how many times I swooped in to save the day. He'd call and I was always there in a flash.

But as Rob got older and even more unpredictable, I became brutally aware of another truth: *you can't save a person who doesn't want to be saved.*

And Rob, the person I loved, made that pretty fuckin' clear too.

Love isn't enough to save the person you love *because* you can't save a person who doesn't want to be saved. When you put those hard truths together, they are destined to cause a world of hurt.

That became abundantly clear to me a few weeks before Rob died. We were walking to the Greek diner that we'd occasionally go to for lunch, and I asked how he was doing. I was expecting the usual one-word answer, but he surprised me by saying that things were really bad and proceeded to tell the story about borrowing money from a loan shark. I wasn't working at the time and had also recently talked myself into "detaching with love," so I told him that I couldn't give him the money.

"I'm not asking you for it," he said in a soft voice, a voice that, in retrospect, screamed that he had made up his mind this time and didn't want to be bailed out. "And even if you had it, I wouldn't take it from you." We then sat down at the diner and ate bacon and eggs while I listened to how he got himself in so deep.

"I don't know what to say," I said after he told me the whole sorrowful story.

"I know. Me neither."

So we both just sat there, not saying anything. Rob was looking at his phone while I fought with myself over the question of whether I should give him the money. My head and heart duked it out for what would be the last time. That afternoon, my head won, not knowing that it, along with my heart, would soon be crushed into a million tiny pieces.

Those shitty truths set Rob free, and there are no words that can undo what he did. Love wasn't enough to save him because he didn't want to be saved. End of sad story.

Love also wasn't enough to save your child—no matter the circumstances of their death—but there's another transformation that happens sometime after they're gone. The world shifts again from revolving around them to revolving around healing yourself.

Although you don't always feel it and oftentimes aren't even aware of it, that's what you're doing now while journeying on the grief recovery road toward becoming an extraordinary parent. It's so easy to lose yourself in the pain and beat yourself up with all the whys, what ifs, and other futile questions.

There's only one answer and it applies to yourself: all you need is love.

· 22 ·

Whys, What Ifs, and
Other Futile Questions

*D*uring the early days after Rob's death, I had a million questions, but they always boiled down to one: why?

Why did Rob do it? Why did he do it the way that he did it? Why did he do it this time and not the other times when he threatened to do it? Why didn't he let me help him this time? Why did he think it would be okay for all of us who loved him to be here without him? Why am I asking these questions when there's nothing we can do to bring him back?

That last question was when I heard the proverbial needle scratch across a record, bringing my monkey mind to a screeching halt. It forced me to look at what I was really doing, specifically, trying to figure out a problem that already had a solution—the most unsatisfactory solution that there ever was.

I was trying to fix what I had always been able to fix with Rob, no matter what awful thing needed fixing. I was trying to think my way out of the pain and make this terrible nightmare go away. I was trying to get my little boy back.

You've probably asked your own whys, what ifs, and other futile questions about your child's death and have likely arrived at similar unsatisfying answers. It's completely normal to ask these questions. We all do it. When you love your child, you can't take any form of *no* for an answer. We're all seeking a way to explain the unexplainable, as if there was an explanation that could possibly provide relief.

Sometimes the answers to your questions are obvious and inevitable, like when your child succumbs to a long illness. Sometimes the answers are elusive—there was an accident or your child was in the wrong place at the wrong time. Sometimes the death is a shock but not

81

a surprise, as it was with Rob. And sometimes you're just suffering so much that you're searching for any answer that will make the torture stop, even for a short while.

So you question your child: *how could you do this to us?* You question yourself: *how could we have let this happen?* You question your faith: *oh Lord, why did you take away our child so soon and what did we do to deserve this?* I knew things were really bad when I started to question God, mainly because I'm not sure if I believe in Him. All the questions in the world, or out of this world, provide little solace.

Much like when everyone consoled you by saying, "There are no words," there are no answers to any of your questions that can change what has happened. A Spanish Inquisition of yourself can help process your loss to a certain extent, but more often than not, it also dredges up feelings of guilt, blame, anger, and sadness, which you then use to punish yourself.

Beating up on yourself keeps you trapped in the past (if only you did . . . whatever you think you should've done to save them) or flings you into the future (if your child was still alive . . . you'd be a grandparent by now). But more than anything, it prevents you from being in the present—the only place that really matters when it comes to working through your grief.

Working through it takes all of your being. It takes strength you didn't know you had. Incessant questioning often weighs you down and gets in the way. It keeps you stuck and prevents you from moving forward. It keeps you trapped inside your head when your heart needs your attention while it slowly begins to heal.

It's your heart that must face what scares you most. It's your heart that grows stronger and braver every time it encounters the grief beast. Your heart isn't interested in any questions because it already knows all the answers.

You need to listen to your heart. You need to trust it. You need to give it time. You need to let it guide you through the darkness. Wherever it takes you is where you need to go. Your heart knows what it needs to do.

• 23 •

Grief Observed

$\mathcal{G}$rief is a lot of things. It's a process. It comes in waves and it comes in stages. It's relentless and can't be controlled. It can last for months, years, or forever. It's incredibly personal and yet universal. It can be complicated, anticipated, distorted, delayed, inhibited, absent, or any combination thereof. All I know is that it sucks and that you must go through it.

There are many common aspects of grief—as anybody who has ever been in a grief support group can attest to—but there's no one size fits all. No two people grieve the same way. Our grief fits us like a glove.

Our children are our children, and our feelings about them are our feelings. Mine are different from yours. My pain is different from yours. The way I hurt is different from the way you hurt.

It's the same deal with love. We all love our children, but we love them in our own way. I loved Rob harder than I've ever loved anyone because that's what he needed. I love Zach easier than I've ever loved anyone because it is the most natural love I've ever known. Simply put, our grief is shaped by the person we loved and lost.

When I got the call that Rob died, I remember initially feeling numb, but really it was more a feeling of resignation, like *what took you so long?* I had been waiting by the phone ever since he was a teenager. I also felt a sense of relief, both for him and for our family. He was no longer struggling with his demons, and we no longer had to worry about the worst thing that could ever happen because it had happened. The intense emotional pain I felt was because I couldn't save him or change him, but more than anything, it was because he was inimitably Rob—the good, the bad, and the ugly, all rolled up into a giant shit ball of grief, hand-crafted just for me by the person I loved and lost.

83

It's been the same way for you. The same, meaning different from everyone else.

Grief is a lot of things, and we all experience it differently and in our own time, but one of the things it most definitely is *not*—in my completely unprofessional opinion—is mental illness. You may sometimes feel crazy and incapacitated; I certainly did. You may be depressed and need meds; I was and did. You may go to a therapist; I went for a solid year. You may be bitter and angry; I was for a short time. You may question your reason for living; I did until I found my answers.

Having said that, I had more questions than answers a few years ago when "prolonged grief" was added to the *Diagnostic and Statistical Manual of Mental Disorders* (DSM for short). It's defined by many of the feelings I've felt, feelings you've felt and perhaps still feel, and it can be diagnosed one year after a loved one's death. Along with designating grief as a type of pathology, the one-year line of demarcation really pissed me off. I don't know about you, but I don't know any bereaved parent who *wasn't* still suffering with many of the "crazy" thoughts and feelings a year after losing a child.

There are certainly some folks who suffer more acutely and are unable to get out of bed and function in the world, and it's great that there are specific psychotherapy treatments to help them. But for the rest of us, things are crazy enough without adding mental illness to the mix.

That day-to-day craziness is only heightened, at least for me, when people compare their grief to mine. First of all, if you've never lost a child, don't tell us about how devastated you were when your mother/father/sister/brother/aunt/uncle/best friend/cat died. Grief is not a contest. There are no winners, only losers.

Second, we residents of Suck City know the score. Comparing your grief to somebody else's makes it suck more, and the last thing we need is for things to suck more than they already suck.

Which is not to say that different flavors of grief don't exist within our own dreadful club. There's a big difference between losing a child at birth and losing a kid when he or she is in their forties or fifties. Grieving for a life that never began is different from grieving for a life that was cut short. The pain is different for each, but it's still the worst pain, because it is yours.

Yet sometimes comparisons happen, albeit inadvertently. About a year into my grief group, one of the dads was having a particularly rough night. His son had died in a freak accident while hiking, and he was missing him hard.

"No father has ever loved their son the way I loved mine," he said before bursting into tears.

When I first heard him say those words, I became indignant. There were other fathers in the room, and we all loved our sons with all of our hearts, and how dare he say that he loved his son more than I loved Rob!

But now I don't think that's what he was saying at all. Now I think he was just expressing his grief, hand-crafted just for him by the person he loved and lost.

· 24 ·

We Were Robbed

$\mathcal{I}$ was recently delighted when I stumbled upon the etymology of the word "bereave." It comes from the Old English *berēafian*, and it basically means "to be robbed." Isn't that great? It tickles me every time I use my son's name as a verb.

We were all robbed. We were robbed of so much that it hurts to think about it, but think about it we must.

You were robbed of a lifetime filled with milestones and memories. You were robbed of your child's smile and of hearing their voice. You were robbed of all the times they'd call with good news. You were robbed of consoling them when they had bad news. You were robbed of becoming best friends and just hanging out with them. You were robbed of walking them down the aisle at their wedding. You were robbed of your grandchildren. You were robbed of growing old with them. You were robbed of being their mom or dad. You were robbed of a fundamental piece of who you are.

The first thing I think about when I think about being robbed is Rob's hugs. As I noted, he gave great hug. For a wiry, little dude (picture a disheveled Kieran Culkin), he really leaned into them with all of his being. Our hugs, when I look back, were the physical manifestation of the tight grip he had on me. Sometimes we held on to each other, and neither of us wanted to let go, right up until the day before he killed himself, leaving nothing for me to hold on to.

Every now and then, I attempt to take back what I was robbed of with a day of magical thinking. You'll see what I mean in a moment, but I highly recommend you give it a try whenever you feel the time is right. All you have to do is close your eyes and imagine your child. They'll take it from there.

On a summery Saturday afternoon, I'll hop on the 405 and pick Rob up at his apartment building in Long Beach. He's waiting out front, smoking a cigarette.

"Yo," he sleepily growls, getting into my car as we bump fists.

"Yo, soup dumplings at Din Tai Fung today?"

"Let's do it."

And so, we do. There's the usual forty-five-minute wait, but we don't care because it's always worth it. I give the hosts my first name and phone number so they can text us when a table is ready, and then Rob and I walk around the mall, catching up on this and that.

"So what's going on at work these days?" I ask, which is generally my first question. "Anything new?"

"The ushe. The restaurant was packed last night. I didn't get home until way late."

"Any good stories?"

"Some celebrity dude who I never heard of came in with a hot girlfriend and people were bugging the shit out of him, asking for autographs and selfies," Rob explains as we walk past a Footlocker. "I had to tell them to chill the fuck out and let the dude eat in peace."

"He must've appreciated it."

"He did. He offered to buy me a pricey whiskey," Rob says. "I told him thanks but no thanks."

"Good for you. How long has it been now?" I ask.

"Closing in on six years."

"Wow, that's amazing!"

Rob just nodded. "You know, I still go to my home group in Hermosa Beach," he says.

"You've been going there forever. Since you first moved to Torrance," I say, momentarily flashing back to the day I took him to his first sober house.

"It's still the best. It sometimes gets really wild, and some folks say some crazy-ass shit," Rob continues, "but I love a whole lot of people in that room."

"Have you spoken with your sponsor lately?" I ask as we sit down on the large, comfy chairs near the entrance to Nordstrom.

"Yeah, I saw him the other week, and we had some eggs at the Greek diner," Rob says. "I hadn't seen him for a while. He's been real busy and having some problems with his wife."

"If you don't mind me asking, what do you guys talk about?"

"It changes each time, but mainly just checking in with him kind of stuff," Rob says while checking texts on his iPhone. "I'm still stuck on step 6. Too much God shit for me."

"I get it. I feel the same way," I say. Then I get choked up for a second. "I'm really proud of you, dude. You've been through some shit. We all have."

"True dat."

"Have you spoken with Zach lately?"

"Yeah, we text all the time. You know, he still sends me new music," Rob says. "But not as much, now that he's married."

"Yeah, that's the way it works. You'll find out someday," I tell him. "Speaking of which, you seeing anyone these days?"

"Maybe."

"Maybe I should mind my own goddamn business?" I ask.

"Something like that."

"Fair enough. When was the last time you spoke with Mom?"

Rob pauses for a moment and looks me in the eyes. "I think it was a few Sundays ago," he says. "She had just come back from a walk on the beach."

"That sounds like Mom."

"Dad, you know I'm not really here with you right now, right?"

"I know, Rob. But can you hang with me for just a little bit longer? Until we get the text that our table is ready?"

"You got it," he says.

"Thank you, sir."

"Hey, that's my line!" Rob says.

"Duh, I know. I say it all the time and every time I say it, I think of you."

"Don't get all weepy on me, Dad."

"Okay, idiot!" I say and we both laugh. It seems just like old times.

"I'll see you when I see you, Rob. I love you."

"Not if I see you first," Rob says and smiles before adding, "I love you, Dad."

This time I just nod. "Those four words, those are the words, right?" Rob asks.

"Right," I mumble through tears. "I just miss you so damn much."

"I get it. Later, father."

"Bye for now, dude," I say before quietly mouthing, "I was just Robbed."

• 25 •

Things Change

*Y*ou've changed. You're different. You're not the same. Grief changes and evolves and so do you. You're not the same person that you were months ago, and you won't be the same person months from now. Grief will continue to reshape you.

It may not feel like things are changing and you may not even notice it because it creeps up on you like old age. You're still heartbroken and can barely function as a human being. You still miss your kid every day, every hour, every minute. You don't cry as much, but when you do, it's hard to stop.

Your world has changed, and you are slowly adapting to it. Remember, grief is a process: "a natural phenomenon marked by gradual changes that lead toward a particular result." Perhaps you've made some of the gradual changes: you've taken a step forward, you've found your people, you don't beat up yourself as much—that's great! I know it doesn't feel great, but it is. Every time you're hit with one of those savage grief waves, it propels you forward, moving you to a healing place. That's the particular result of this particular process.

The thing is, it's difficult if not impossible to notice the changes that are happening, because you can't see the forest for the trees. That's where time comes in. Your perspective shifts with time, and your feelings undergo their own metamorphosis. Once you get a little distance away from the darkness, it becomes easier to see yourself in a new light.

I didn't realize how much I had changed until close to a year after Rob died. It was difficult to imagine that something good could come from his death, but I became more patient and forgiving. I let a lot more things slide. I became softer, almost all of my edges had worn away. I became less scared and more openhearted than I've ever been in my life. I was spending more time in the here and now and less time revisiting the past. I focused on the things that really mattered to me—mainly, loving all the people in my heart—and I no longer let petty matters ruin my day.

Which is not to say that I wasn't still capable of being an asshole, but I was a kinder, gentler asshole. Moreover, for the first time in my life, I began thinking about how I could help others, which led me a few years later to become a volunteer grief counselor and coach. I was beginning to see the light.

And I've discovered that the changes keep on coming, and I learn a little more each time they do. I suspect that they will continue, and I welcome that with open arms.

It's inevitable that things change when your child dies. They cannot possibly stay the same. And by now you know that the changes are custom made. Some of the changes are by choice, some just seemingly happen, and some feel like larger forces have intervened.

I asked Caryn how she has changed since Rob's death, and this is what she had to say.

So for reasons I can't explain, there are days when I wake up and things are very routine. I brush my teeth, shower, work, my son passed away, I have to go food shopping, mundane things like that. And then other times, I'll be in my car on my way to yoga, and it feels like I'm having an out-of-body experience. Profound sadness and disbelief and hopelessness. And then after a few moments, I move on. I know how to handle my grief now. I have more control over it, but if I allow myself to "go there" it is still very raw.

More than anything, Rob's death has given me a new perspective on life. I feel like my patience with minutiae is nonexistent, and I compare my loss to everything. Therefore, I find it hard to be compassionate. When someone tells me about an inconvenience in their life, I think to myself, "Wow, how lucky are you that that's your biggest problem today!"

By the same token, I've become completely vulnerable and empathetic to people who are suffering what I consider to be "real" loss. I want to hug them a little longer. I want them to know how much I understand their pain and that they are not alone, that life changes and the pain changes with it.

Finally, the happiness of my living son and, well, you, *are paramount to me. I am acutely aware of how I feel about peace and joy for both of you guys.*

As for myself, I'm not sure what the point is in anything most days.

There's one other change that feels akin to magic, like this change is somehow trying to replace the piece of you that's missing. It happens a little further down the extraordinary parent road, and it could be the most significant change of all—when you discover your purpose and begin to live a more meaningful life.

· 26 ·

The Things They Left Behind

$\mathcal{I}$ don't have any of Rob's stuff. He didn't have very much and I'm not sure what I would do with any of it if I had it. I've never been particularly sentimental and I don't think any of his things would make me feel any better or any worse about him not being here. The things he left behind are not the things I choose to hold on to.

But that's just me. Many other bereaved parents have many other feelings about what they should do with their kids' things. For some, the thought of throwing away anything that belonged to their child is unbearable. Others can barely tolerate going through their child's belongings because reliving the memories attached to them is equally heartbreaking.

And then there are parents who immediately rid themselves of their child's stuff so that they're not constantly reminded of their colossal loss, while still others leave their kid's room perfectly intact because it's comforting and reminds them of what could've been.

I won't tell you what to do, but whatever you choose to do (or not to do) and whenever you do it (or don't do it) is fine. There are no rules or deadlines when it comes to this kind of thing and my only advice is to follow your heart.

What I can tell you is that deciding what to do with your child's stuff is painful, in the same way it's painful to face all the things that scare you the most. It's also a necessary step of the grief work that needs to happen on the way toward acceptance and healing. As grim as this sounds, you know you're doing the work when it hurts.

There's a good chance that your feelings about your child's things may shift over time. If you've been holding on tight or afraid to let go, you may feel a bracing relief when you begin to shed some of their stuff, like taking a breath of the cool night air. Time, as you may already have discovered, will often answer many of the questions you're struggling with.

What you end up doing with your child's belongings is, of course, up to you. You may want to give away some of it to friends and family and cherry-pick meaningful items to stash away for yourself. You may want to donate some of their clothes and gear to charities and feel good knowing that somebody else's less fortunate kid will benefit from the things your child left behind.

Other than totally gutting us, Rob didn't leave much in his wake. The first time I went to his apartment after he died, I was looking for a suicide note and didn't find one. I returned a few weeks later to collect a bunch of his old T-shirts for Caryn, who was going to have them made into a memorial quilt.

I went straight into his bedroom and emptied the drawers, grabbing his faves—Rob's life story told in medium-size T-shirts. They included Columbine Physical Education, Slightly Stoopid, Kottonmouth Kings, and everybody's favorite, Ante Christ, featuring a forlorn-looking Jesus sitting at a poker table.

I stuffed about twenty of them into a trash bag and then dug around for other artifacts. There was a manila envelope on the bed, and I got excited, hoping it might contain new information, but I was immediately disappointed when I saw it was just a dozen or so resumes I had printed out for him a few weeks prior when his internet access was turned off. I went from room to room looking through the tragic rubble and when I walked into the kitchen, I just shook my head. There were his stupid lighters.

Displayed neatly on a tray on the countertop, the lighters looked out of place next to all the garbage surrounding them. Rob had more than two hundred BIC disposable lighters, and I never understood why he was so proud of this oddball collection. It always made me a little sad that this was one of his prized possessions. I didn't know what to do with them, so I called Zach.

"Yo, I'm at Rob's place cleaning up his shit, and I just found those stupid lighters. Should I grab them?" I asked.

"Everybody knows about Rob's lighters, Dad," he said. "You don't need to take them."

So I left them behind. A few weeks later, the building manager called to say that she had a box of Rob's personal belongings that she thought I might want, so I drove to Long Beach for the last time.

There was a stack of unopened mail, most of it from healthcare providers that I had signed him up for a few days before he died. His high school yearbook was also in there next to two small wooden boxes with sliding bottoms that turned out to be the ashes of his two sugar gliders that he had with him in Binghamton. There was a final warning notice for an unpaid ticket he'd received a few days before Christmas that cited him for eating, drinking, and smoking in Downtown Long Beach. Long Beach needn't worry about Rob anymore.

There were also a handful of money order receipts, a California license plate, a birthday card from Aunt Robin, four more tickets (issued in New York for driving while intoxicated), his lease, a notice that gave him three days to pay rent or move out, his birth certificate from the Missouri Department of Health, a number of earnings statements from the casino, a broken pocket watch, and a key ring with a twenty-four-hour "one day at a time" camel AA chip.

At the bottom of the box, I found four loose pages that looked like they'd been ripped out of a spiral notebook. At the top of the first page was the heading "Fear Inventory." Dated 2/19/18—almost exactly a year before Rob died—it was written in his barely legible scrawl and divided into three columns: "What am I afraid of," "Why," and "Where self-reliance has failed me." This was an exercise connected to the fourth step in AA, in which you're asked to make a fearless moral inventory of yourself, basically identifying your own weaknesses. It was the last two items on the list that went straight to my heart:

What am I afraid of: Not having kids.
Why: If you don't have kids, there's no one to carry on your memory . . . who you were, and the family name.
Where self-reliance has failed me: I never wanted to have kids before and now that I do, I realize I missed an excellent opportunity.

What am I afraid of: Not being a good father.

Why: My father was an excellent father. He provided my family with everything I needed and more. . . . The moral lessons he taught me. . . . How can I be as good a father as him?

Where self-reliance has failed me: I can barely take care of myself let alone a kid.

Like I said, the things Rob left behind are not the things I choose to hold on to.

· 27 ·

Thirty-Second Time-Out

Let me say it once more for emphasis: we all experience grief differently and in our own time. Our journey is our journey (and yes, I hate that melodramatic cliché, too!). My hope is that you recognize some of the feelings I've felt, but I'm keenly aware that some of you may not. Maybe you've felt them at different times than I've felt them. Maybe you haven't felt them yet. And for sure, you've felt things that I haven't felt.

That's why I need to take this thirty-second time-out. (I have one more remaining in the second half of this book.) It hit me that some of the things I'm suggesting may seem wildly off base, totally foreign, or just plain facile. It also hit me that you may not be feeling the way I felt after Rob died, and some of my suggestions may make you want to hit me. Fair enough. Sometimes I want to hit myself too.

We all know that those hits are relentless. Grief pummels us like nothing else until we're finally strong enough and self-aware enough to say enough is enough and to move on with the rest of our lives.

Getting there takes time. Grief is all about time. It takes time to process the loss of any loved one, and it takes the longest amount of time when that loved one is your baby boy or girl.

Right from the jump, it feels like you're frozen in time along with your child, and then it takes time to unthaw before you can start your grief journey. It then takes some more time to gain perspective and see things differently. It takes even more time to change. It takes a long time to heal. It takes an even longer time to find joy.

Some people get there faster than others. Some people take their own sweet time. And some people never get there. It's all about time, but it's also about how you use it. Time heals but it doesn't heal by itself, which is why I humbly suggest using it wisely throughout this book. Even if we're in different grief time zones.

Okay, time back in.

• 28 •

Parts of You

One part of you knows that you must go on with your life, while another part doesn't ever want to get out of bed. One part of you feels like you did everything possible to save your child, while another part takes you to task for not having done enough. One part of you believes that you were the best parent a child could ever have, while another part questions how you could possibly be the best parent when you failed to keep your child alive.

One part of you accepts the reality of your loss, while another part remains lost in disbelief. One part of you acknowledges that love never dies and that grief lasts a lifetime, while another part wonders how you could possibly continue to live like this. One part of you understands that enduring the worst thing that could ever happen to a parent makes you a stronger person, while another part asks how you can be stronger when a piece of you is missing and can never be replaced.

One part of you has begun to process your grief by facing what scares you the most, while another part simply ignores it. One part of you has stopped crying all the time and feels a tiny bit better, while another part suffers an intense sadness that will never go away. One part of you doesn't allow the loss to define you, while another part feels like the poster child for bereaved parents who are endlessly pitied.

One part of you is slowly letting go of denial, guilt, anger, and fear, while another part is drowning in an ocean of sorrow. One part of you has been able to experience joy again, however short-lived, while another part feels terribly guilty about it. One part of you has become a warrior, while another part is exhausted and ready to give up.

One part of you is hopeful that you'll survive your tragic loss as so many have before you, while another part is certain that nobody has ever experienced the depth of pain you're living through. One part of you is certain that nothing can ever hurt you again, while another part is an open wound that will never heal. One part of you takes great comfort in your faith, while another part admonishes God for taking away the most cherished gift He ever gave to you.

One part of you is becoming yourself again, while another part feels that the best part of yourself is gone forever. One part of you has stopped torturing yourself by asking unanswerable questions, while another part stays up all night trying to answer them in vain. One part of you needs to be strong for your other children, while another part secretly fears for their lives.

One part of you has changed and evolved with your grief, while another part is scared that if you change too much, you'll lose the connection with your child. One part of you senses that what you're feeling is exactly what you should be feeling and that you'll feel differently in the future, while another part views the future as meaningless.

One part of you realizes that juggling all these complex and paradoxical feelings is just part of the grieving process—that you can hold opposing thoughts at the same time—while another part, after making a fuss, reluctantly agrees.

One part of you concedes that the whole is greater than the sum of its parts, while another part still wonders how to become whole again.

· 29 ·

Say Hello to My Sad Little Friends

*D*espite being misunderstood for many years, we've all become well-acquainted with the now classic Kübler-Ross five stages of grief: denial, anger, bargaining, depression, and acceptance. When you add 'em all up, you've supposedly learned how to live with the loss of your loved one, that is, the stupid fuckin' idiot. That was Anger talking, and since I don't want him to have the last word, it's time to hear from all of my sad little friends.

Hi, I'm Denial, but I'd never admit it. I was the first to hear the horrible news and I coined the phrase "shocked but not surprised." I remember my survival instinct kicking in and then going numb, because that's what I do best. From the moment Larry got the call, Rob's death felt surreal: how could his little boy be gone? Larry woke each morning thinking that he was inside a bad dream. Nothing made any sense to him, and I'm not sure how he made it through each day.

I was the first responder—nature's way of letting in only as much as Larry could handle. Unfortunately, Larry's nature only allowed me to hang out with him for about a week.

That's when I took over the grieving process. I'm Anger. Duh! At first, I couldn't believe what the little asshole had done—whether it was impulsive, premeditated, who gives a shit?—because any way you slice it, he had to know how much it would fuck us up forever, and that made me boiling mad. How could he be so selfish after all we had done for him, after all we had been through together?

And then I raged against the God machine for allowing this tragedy to happen—I believe my exact words were "vengeful motherfucker"—until I remembered that Larry's not even sure if he believes in Him.

I tried to stay furious at Rob, I really, really did. I thought it would give us strength. I knew it was a way to keep Rob close, a way to cope with the nothingness of his loss while also expressing the intensity of Larry's love for the stupid moron. But, damn it, I wasn't invited to stick around for very long, either. Which royally pissed me off and still does! Ugh!

Bargaining here. Rob didn't give me much of a chance to negotiate with him while he was alive, so now I just wheel and deal with Larry's pain. I'm not as angry as the previous guy or as sad as the guy you'll hear from next, and I come and go as I please, as most of us do. Grief and mourning offer no discounts or giveaways. As I'm sure you've come to realize, everyone must pay the highest price.

I generally work with what some people think is a rather pesky partner named Guilt. All the whys and what-ifs? That's him! It took a long while until Larry finally showed us the door, and that was after countless confrontations with my irksome colleague, especially late at night, right before Lar fell asleep.

Hello darkness, my old friend, I've come to talk with you again. That's about the best joke and transition I can muster. Cut me a break! I'm Depression, not Rodney freaking Dangerfield. I've been around from time to time, way before Rob died, way before he was even born. I'm the all-encompassing fog of sadness, the emptiness in Larry's soul, and, as he so expressively puts it, the space in his heart that will never close.

At the same time, I had never felt so necessary in all his life. I was the biggest—and shittiest—stage of the entire grief cryfest, but I was also the most important. That thought would make me happy if I wasn't so damn sad. I offered no shortcuts in our travels through hell, and the pain was unimaginable. As if that weren't enough, I demanded to be endured. I was the sorrowful music of his heartbreak (composed and performed by Bill Evans), and Larry and I slow danced alone until the healing finally kicked in. At least that was what the next guy told me, although I'm not sure if I ever really believed him.

Welcome! My name's Acceptance, and Tom Hanks would probably play me in the movie version of the Kübler-Ross model. So here's the thing: I was trying to cheer up Depression. He's such a sad guy, with all the weeping and gloom and doom, but I meant what I said about healing. I arrived a few months after Larry had been cracked open by Rob's death, and I'm the true guardian of his soul. I had invited Denial to help ease the pain early on, and then I let Anger take over so Larry could blow off some steam. Bargaining barged in with his annoying partner in crime, and those pests were a bit more difficult to ditch. And let's just say Depression and I came to an understanding.

When Larry talks about being "forever changed," he's talking about me. I helped him cope with Rob not being here and with recognizing the reasons why he's not. Like many of his past therapists, I've encouraged him to learn how to sit with uncomfortable feelings. We mainly talked about Rob no longer struggling with his demons and finally being at peace and how his spirit will live in our hearts for all time.

Some people, maybe even you, are bound to misinterpret my name. I know it sounds kind of hopeful, but the truth is I can't make anything feel okay for Lar because losing Rob will never feel okay. I can, however, continue to help him heal and live without Rob. I have to. And I will. We don't have any other choice.

• 30 •

Putting in the Work

$\mathcal{O}$ne night about a year into my grief group, I mentioned that I had been feeling slightly optimistic for the first time because I was "putting in the work." My friend Vic, who was still struggling with the loss of his son Sam, asked, "What exactly is 'the work'?" And I said, "You know, the work! The stuff we're all doing right now in here." I couldn't explain it any more than that back then, but I can now.

When you're just sitting around thinking about your child, you're putting in the work. When you're in the shower crying, you're putting in the work. When you journal about your poor baby, you're putting in the work. When you're talking about your kid with a friend, you're putting in the work. When you're in a grief group, you're putting in the work. When you're talking to a therapist, you're putting in the work. Putting in the work is how you process your grief.

Putting in the work is a full-time job that starts you off at minimum wage. It's dirty, messy, and the ultimate heavy lift. It can be a total grind and it definitely hurts, but this is what I've been talking about every time I say that you must go *through* grief. The biggest secret about grief isn't a secret at all. It's actually the most obvious thing in the world— the *only* way you can go through grief is by putting in the work. And when the work is done—make that *almost* done, because the work can last forever—you'll realize that you've gained a wealth of knowledge no money can buy.

Putting in the work leaves no stone unturned. It examines all of your questions with a fine-tooth comb. It unbottles your oceanic feelings and allows you to express them with whomever you trust to share them with. The more you can unburden yourself, the more you can unravel your traumatic stories and reframe them, the more you can begin to accept the things you can't change, the faster you'll make it through the grief tunnel.

You can't rush things, you can't jump over it, and try as you might, you can't really avoid it. If you want to deny it for a while, that's your prerogative. It will still be there, fresh as a daisy, whenever you're ready to face it.

Putting in the work takes a lot of time and effort because there's just so much to sort out. From accepting the reality of the loss, to processing the pain, to adjusting to the world without Rob, to integrating the loss and moving forward with the rest of my life took me about two years. It might take you more time or less, depending on how your child died, your relationship with them, and your overall willingness to open yourself up, which includes being open to pain. That last part is essential because it's pointless to put in the work if you can't feel the pain it produces. The pain, counterintuitively, helps you recover and heal.

It helps you to make sense of all the things that haven't made sense before and is ultimately a stabilizing force. Saying the things that have been left unsaid will come as a great relief that can only propel you forward. Facing the things that scare you the most will imbue you with a sense of fearlessness that you could never imagine.

It's not for the faint of heart. It will be the hardest thing you've ever done in your life. It helps you break down everything you're struggling with—emotionally, behaviorally, cognitively, spiritually—as if you were peeling away the layers of an onion, which, as we all know, is certain to make you cry.

Sometimes it's like playing Whac-a-Mole: you come to accept that there was nothing you could have done to prevent your child's death, and then some uncertain decision you made while they were alive resurfaces. So you whack down that one, and two or three new issues rear their ugly heads. And even though you're the one doing the whacking, it often feels like you're the mole.

Whacking down each troubling question or uncomfortable feeling that pops up is putting in the work, and as you move through your grief, you get better and faster at the whacking, and once you've laid most of those little bastards to rest, you can finally crawl into bed and get a good night's sleep.

· 31 ·

The Larry Show

$\mathcal{I}$'ve been in and out of therapy for more than half of my life, and I used to joke that I've made several therapists rich beyond their wildest dreams. I've mostly sought treatment during times of crisis—when my mom died, when my marriage was crumbling, and most recently, well, you know most recently. I've always liked the process of talk therapy, and I also liked that for fifty or so minutes a week, it's *The Larry Show* starring Larry, featuring tonight's special guest—Larry.

I'm still fond of the chatty part of *The Larry Show*, but grappling with the loss of Rob just didn't feel like something I could talk my way out of. I interviewed a bunch of different therapists before I found Katarina, and the first thing I said to each of them, in a somewhat challenging borderline-asshole tone, was, "There's nothing you can do to make me feel any better right now, so what the hell am I doing here, and how the hell are you going to help me?"

I liked Katarina's answer the best. "I'm here to listen and to get to know you," she said matter-of-factly, in an accent I couldn't place until she told me that she's from Croatia. It was at the end of our first session that she introduced me to the idea of EMDR.

EMDR is an acronym for the mouthful that's eye movement desensitization and reprocessing. It's a nontraditional therapeutic treatment used primarily with people who have experienced some horribly fucked-up shit (which is Larry talk for "trauma"), and it's supposed to work a lot faster than the more conventional gabfest.

With EMDR, you're basically reliving your trauma in small doses while being distracted by doing specific eye movements and something called "bilateral stimulation." There are several theories about why it's effective. It's kinda like rewiring your emotions but without feeling like you're going to become a creepy Scientologist.

Despite the knee-jerk skepticism built into every New York Jew, I was open to trying it because I was open to anything that may somehow relieve any of my pain and sadness. Enough talk, it was time for action.

I remember sitting under a jasmine tree in the backyard behind Katarina's office, and after the usual pleasantries, she handed me two small green paddles, one for each hand. A mild, vibrating sensation began to bounce from one hand to the other (that's the bilateral stimulation, which at first sounded to me like an old George Carlin joke), and after a few minutes I didn't even notice it. This is where the reprocessing of traumatic memories comes in. It's supposedly a more natural way for the brain to handle those memories . . . either that or total nonsense in which nothing really happens.

Katarina then instructed me to close my eyes and imagine myself somewhere safe, tranquil, and beautiful.

"Where are you?" she asked after giving me a moment.

"I'm on a beach in Malibu right before sunset," I said, instantly aware of what a cliché that was.

"Okay, good. Now I want you to imagine someone who can comfort you, like a maternal type of figure," she instructed. "It could be a fictional character from a book, movie, or TV show. Or someone you know, someone who can take care of you."

I had to think about it for a minute. "Okay, got it," I said.

"Who is it?"

"Meryl Streep! I just figured she can play anybody."

"Good. Fine. Okay, so now I want you to picture someone who can protect you. Someone who is strong and able to fight for you. A defender or superhero. Again, it could be anyone, fictional or real."

"Hmm. . . . Lemme think on it a moment. Oh! Yeah! Okay!"

"Who is it?"

"Harry Potter! He's perfect to tussle with 'He Who Shall Not Be Named'!"

"Ha! Good! Now think of someone who is very wise, someone with a lot of wisdom who can give you sensible advice."

"That's easy," I said. "My close friend, John Birmingham!"

"All right. So now I want you to picture each of them coming to sit down next to you on the beach. First, Meryl, then Harry, then John,"

Katarina continued. "I want you to sit together and just enjoy the sunset with them. Really, whatever you want them to do is fine. Just breathe naturally and take pleasure in their company. I'm going to leave you there and not say anything for a while."

And that's pretty much what I did for the next twenty or so minutes, until I sensed that our time might be up and opened my eyes.

"How are you feeling?" Katarina asked. "What was that like for you?"

"Um . . . it was interesting. They were all on the beach, but Harry Potter was too hot and had to take off his robe. Meryl and John got along famously, as I knew they would," I playfully answered. "But really, since I'm a word person rather than a visual thinker, I imagined each of them saying something different, and then I started to repeat what they were saying like a mantra."

"What were they saying to you?"

"Well, Meryl was saying, 'I love you, little boy!' Harry was saying, 'Nothing can ever hurt you!' And John was saying, 'Just be you!' And that's what I was hearing in my head the entire time I had my eyes closed, over and over again. And the funny thing was that the sun never set. It remained that soft, yellowish-red light, and that's sort of the way I felt."

"Wow! I'm impressed! You're a natural at this," Katarina said.

We went on like this for months, and each and every time we did EMDR, I thought someone was going to burst out from another room holding a hidden camera and tell me that I'd been punked. But it must've had some positive effects because after about a year, Katarina finally kicked me out of the nest. She said enough already; I had done the work and it was time for me to live my life. No therapist had ever said that to me before and I will always love her for that.

• 32 •

Trigger Happy

$\mathcal{A}$s I'm sure you've come to know, we are a tightly wound group that is easily triggered. There are the obvious ones like the anniversary of your child's death, their birthday, or any number of tragic milestones and holidays. We know that they're coming each year, and we prepare ourselves for how we think we're going to feel, which is very often worse than what actually happens. For the first few years, these occasions simply suck, and then, as time goes by, they begin to suck slightly less.

Those triggers stay with you, and you'll continue to manage them the best that you can. Then there are the ones that come out of nowhere and feel like guided missiles aimed straight at your heart.

You're suddenly crying harder than you've cried in months, and it feels almost like it did during the early days after your child's death. You can't believe that you're feeling this intense sadness again, this terrible reminder (as if you need reminding!) that your child is gone. It's the most unpleasant time travel imaginable.

Anything that evokes painful memories of your child can be a trigger. I don't need to list them all here, since they can be almost anything and they're different for each of us, but triggers generally have one thing in common: they often indicate that there's still grief work to be done.

My big trigger was soup dumplings, the dish Rob and I liked best. The first few times I tried to eat them after he died, I felt sick to my stomach. There was a foul aftertaste that matched the nauseating feeling I got whenever I thought about never seeing him again. I couldn't eat them for months. Every time I tried, it brought me back to the day before he killed himself, a Proustian madeleine that tasted like death warmed over.

Then one day, on Katerina's advice, I tried to Jedi mind trick myself and reframe my lunch memories with Rob. I went back to Din Tai Fung, the scene of the crime, grabbed a seat at the bar, and ordered what we usually ordered. Every time I reached for a pork soup dumpling and dipped it in the mix of soy sauce, vinegar, and ginger, I thought of Rob and me quietly sitting there together, happily stuffing our faces.

Whatever was going on in Rob's life at the time—to be sure, there was always something going on—would vanish while we were eating at Din Tai Fung, which seemed to add a little bit of tasty magic to the meals we shared. I looked back on all the lunches that we had together, just hanging out and enjoying each other's company, while associating the deliciousness and my love of this food with the deliciousness and love of my son. And, I'm happy to report, I've been gorging on pork *xiao long bao* ever since.

Your triggers are clearly different from mine and may not be as tasty. It could be a photo or song or something on TV. It could be a smell or a sound or any other sense memory that hits you out of the blue and makes you feel the acute pain you thought you were pretty much done with. The pain, however, is affirming that it's not quite done with you.

And as brutal and upsetting as it feels, you may just want to sit with whatever emotions are stirred up and let them wash over you. Try to glean any new insights into why they're making you feel the way you feel. Once you recognize what button is being pushed, you can learn how to cope with it and eventually resolve any loose grief ends. You can choose to embrace or recalibrate the experience, as I did, that's up to you, but the important thing is that you face it. The pain of being triggered is just like any other grief pain—you can learn from it and also gather strength from it. It's all part of putting in the work.

Not many things trigger me these days. When I'm running a grief group for bereaved parents, I'm able to compartmentalize my own feelings from the upsetting stories being told in the room, although I do feel a special kinship with fathers who have lost a son to suicide.

You would think the very word would possibly set me off, but it doesn't. When I hear someone inadvertently say that they had a rough day and feel like "blowing their brains out" or "killing themselves," I get what they're saying, and I don't immediately picture Rob doing what he did. There have even been days when I've said those shitty words myself.

The one thing that still triggers me, and I suspect always will, is hearing Rob's voice. I have only one saved voicemail from a few years before he died. It's just Rob saying, "Hey, happy birthday. Gimme a call back. Love you. Bye."

It makes me weep whenever I play it, triggering poignant thoughts of our lifetime together and the love we shared. And if that's also a sign of unfinished grief work, I'll happily listen to Rob's birthday message until the day I die.

· 33 ·

Three Women

*G*rief puts an inconceivable strain on any relationship. It brings some people together and tears others apart. When Rob died, I became closer with my ex-wife than ever before and broke up with my girlfriend on the one-year anniversary of his death.

I've been fortunate to have loved and still love three women in my life, but only one has shared my grief. Caryn and I held onto each other in our inevitable heartbreak because it was ours and ours alone. We adopted Rob, raised him, went through the wringer with him, broke up because of him, and then buried him. We consoled each other during the worst pain in our lives and have given each other hope when things seemed completely hopeless.

I did most of my worrying about Rob with Caryn, the first woman I had ever loved, and our corresponding anxieties fed off each other until we were completely debilitated and finally uncoupled. And then we continued to worry about Rob separately. I can't imagine any parents who worried about their kid as much as we did.

We've had our ups and downs in the years since Rob passed away, but we always find our way back to each other. We live on opposite coasts and talk every Sunday. We know nothing we say about Rob will change anything, yet we say it anyway because we know that we understand each other better than anyone else can understand us. We've known each other for more than forty years and that's a lot of knowing. We'll always love and be there for each other, and if that's not the very definition of family, I don't know what is.

I've always felt terribly guilty for inflicting Rob on Maura, the second woman I ever loved. She was mostly great about it, and they got along well, but as time wore on, her patience—understandably—began to wear thin. Having Rob in our house fundamentally changed the way we lived. Two's company, three's a crowd, and to make matters worse, the dynamic had shifted to Rob and me being the twosome.

I'm pretty sure that's what annoyed her most. Rob had once again become the center of my universe. From the day he was born to the day he died, Rob always came first. Rob came before Zach, Rob came before Caryn, Rob came before Maura, and I couldn't/wouldn't/didn't do a damn thing about it. Rob was a total eclipse of a son. I know how messed up that sounds, but that's just the way it was.

Caryn and Zach lived with Rob for most of his life and knew the deal. Maura hadn't signed up for any of that. We met in Park Slope, fell in love, and then moved to LA together, where we were happy for several years until Rob descended on us like a plague of locusts. From that day on, we gradually disconnected from each other, and things went further south after Rob suddenly disconnected from us.

No matter how hard I tried to share my grief with Maura, she was always outside of the mournful circle, and in retrospect, I'm not sure how hard I really tried. She was there for me with an open heart, but like I said, there was only one person whom I could truly grieve with, and Maura, who had never been a parent, became the odd man out.

Our breakup wasn't so much a breakup as it was a cloud of smoke that slowly dissipated until nothing was there. I'd gone to New York for the unveiling of Rob's headstone in early March 2020 while Maura went to Boston to visit her sisters. When I got back to Venice, I was diagnosed with COVID-19 and learned that Maura had it too.

I remember talking to her one night soon after, and although my memory is fuzzy, I think I said something like, "Everyone in the world right now is with the people they love, and I'm here alone in Venice, and you're in Boston with your sisters. I guess that says it all."

It said more than I realized. Maura, who turned out to be suffering from long COVID, never came back to LA. We're still good friends who love each other, and she'll always be in my heart.

I now live with the third and last woman I will ever love, sweet Jane, in Venice, just steps from the beach. Of all the women in my life, I think Janie, who has been sober for many years, would've truly been able to help Rob. At least that's what I'd like to imagine when we're sitting on the sand together, watching another beautiful sunset, hand in hand.

· 34 ·

Answers from the Great Beyond

$\mathcal{I}$f you've never gone to a psychic or medium before, here's your chance. You don't have to believe in any of this otherworldly phenomena. I didn't believe until I desperately needed to.

I went to see Fleur twice—once before Rob died, for what's known as a "life reading" (Fleur is a psychic) and later for a "spirit reading" (she's also a medium). I'm pretty sure she's the real deal, but feel free to draw your own conclusions.

What follows is an edited and annotated sampling from our second session (Fleur's comments are in italics). Keep in mind that I didn't tell her anything about Rob other than that he had taken his own life.

I see your father has also passed. I feel your son coming in on the right-hand side, your father comes in on the left, and they stand side by side. It feels to me that, prior to his passing, your father hasn't done right by you. He's acknowledging that. But he was there with your son to assist in making it an easy transition.

Right off the bat, I just lost it. I had never cried for my father before, but hearing that he was there to help Rob touched me so deeply that I forgave him for a lifetime of transgressions.

Your son talks about receiving help for sobriety, and this doesn't just feel like AA, but also rehabilitation centers.

She's in the right ballpark, but Rob never went to rehab. He did live in a few sober houses and I think that's what she was referring to.

There's the recognition that, as an adult, he goes back to living with a parent for a while.

He lived with Caryn for more than a year and with me for about four months.

He wants to thank you for it.

You're welcome, dude.

It doesn't appear to me when he passes that it's simply an overdose. There may have been drug use or addiction in the past, but the way he chooses to go feels more deliberate to me.

Now she's getting warmer.

He wasn't sober at the time, so I don't really experience the passing because I feel very disassociated with him at that moment, but . . . he must have had a gun registered to him.

He definitely had a gun; its provenance remains unknown.

It would have been a surprise to people that he had one. That doesn't feel like information anyone is aware of.

That sounds about right. He once mentioned that he was thinking about getting a gun to protect himself from a loan shark, but the subject never came up again. When Rob said that he was "thinking about" doing something, it usually meant that he had already done it.

I feel like this is planned for quite some time . . . that the purpose of this gun is for that reason, nothing else. He hides that and puts on a bright face.

That's right on the money. I had never seen him look happier than when he and Zach were at my house on Christmas, a few months before he killed himself.

He's aware of that false presentation of himself and doesn't want you or his mom or his sibling to feel that there is any sign that was missed. He didn't want anyone to know.

That was when I knew she was talking with Rob.

At some point, he was prescribed drugs for depression, which I don't feel like he was taking even though he said he was.

Rob got into a few legal jams when he was seventeen, and seeing a therapist and taking meds was part of his probation agreement. Years later, he admitted that he never took any of them.

He places sunflowers all around his mom.

Caryn had told me that she sees sunflowers almost everywhere she goes! When the two of us visited Rob at the cemetery some months after this reading, there was a giant one right next to where he's buried.

He's talking about you listening to music of his . . .

True.

He's been beside you as you listened to it. . . . He keeps making me feel that no one could have changed what he did, that he had made up his mind. He had a real struggle with addiction, which he does find relief from.

This made me cry.

Did you ever get matching tattoos? There's a feeling of being tied together by a tattoo.

Totally accurate: Caryn and two of Rob's friends got matching four-leaf clover tattoos, which Rob had on his left hand. Caryn and Zach also got "Life Rolls On" tats, like one that Rob had on his forearm. I had one with the kids' names on my shoulder and then got "You are the sand, little boy, and I will always be the water" tattooed on my left forearm. And Caryn subsequently got a sunflower tattoo. So big yes on Rob ink.

At the funeral, there were plans to say certain words that you did not say?

This gave me chills. I totally changed the eulogy that I had prepared on the plane to New York. The whole thing just felt too performative, as if I were going to deliver a speech written by Aaron Sorkin.

He was right there with you at the time. He makes me feel that you wore something very unlike yourself. He's like, "Why is he wearing a tie?" He found what you were wearing to be . . . ridiculous.

That sounded so much like Rob that I felt like I was actually talking with him.

He wants you to know he had an amazing childhood. It feels like there's a lot of joy there to be found.

There was definitely joy, but it's interesting that he didn't mention the many non-joyful parts. I guess every family's history is a variation on *Rashomon.*

He's acknowledging that you've started speaking to him quite regularly. I know he likes that. It feels like it's on a nightly basis, and he's there with you every time. It may sound silly, but he also wants you to look for feathers.

All true, especially about the feathers, which I'll talk about soon.

Does his mom live somewhere where she would see wild rabbits? Keep on the lookout for bunnies; he's going to send those to her.

I told Caryn about the bunnies, but she hadn't seen any yet. Maybe he's too busy with the sunflowers.

It feels like he wants his departure ultimately to strengthen the bonds in the family, and right now that's not happening. There's a sense of really needing to hold your people close.

Good advice, dude. Much appreciated.

At this point in our session, Fleur asked if I had any questions for Rob, and the first thing I wanted to know was why he didn't ask me to help him at the end.

He just doesn't see a way out and doesn't feel like you helping would change the pattern that's in place. His decision is steadfast. He wouldn't have let anyone change his mind.

Fair enough. I then asked about the night he killed himself and mentioned that there were two people with him.

I feel like the two people there called for help immediately. I don't feel they're responsible. It just feels like it also takes them by surprise.

That's what I was getting at, so asked and answered.

There's some sort of thing here where he is premeditating it, doesn't mean to do it in that moment, but is playing it out in his head.

"Accidentally on purpose" is how I'd been thinking about it.

I also feel that, when he's doing it, the two people who are there aren't necessarily seeing him do it. He's on his own and they're talking in the corner, and they only hear it. . . . He's messing around with it, but with the intention in the future, not in that moment.

This was a better explanation than what was in the police report. It all made a kind of heartbreaking sense. I had two final questions. First, does he know how much we all love him?

Absolutely. There's a huge familial connection here. . . . There isn't that feeling of abandonment that you would have felt with your father.

This also made me cry. Last question: how does he feel about me writing about him?

It feels like his mom has hesitation, but he's okay with it. He says you're going to get some heat from her.

Accurate.

When the reading was over, I thanked Fleur and then she said one more thing about suicide that has stayed with me ever since: "The soul knows when it's time to go."

As much as it hurts me to say it, I believe Rob's sweet soul knew.

· 35 ·

The Soul Knows When It's Time to Go

*T*rying to make sense of suicide is a fool's errand, and I've been that fool ever since Rob died. Losing any relative to suicide is traumatic, but it's particularly devastating for parents, who feel like a failure in the most important job of their lives.

I tortured myself for the better part of two years, asking the same questions over and over again—is there anything we could've done to prevent Rob from doing what he did?

In the days and weeks after his death, the answer seemed obvious: *yes!* For God's sake, I was with him the day before he killed himself. Shouldn't I have picked up on warning signs? Shouldn't I have asked him if he was depressed, or how he was sleeping, or if he was still going to AA meetings? Shouldn't I have offered to give him money, or get him meds, or take him to the emergency room like I did previously? Shouldn't I have done something? Anything?

Shouldn't we have been able to nip his mental illness in the bud when he was a little boy and get him on the right combo platter of drugs to smooth him out? Shouldn't we have thrown him into rehab, where he could've received proper treatment and then maybe he would've turned his life around? Shouldn't we have done more? How could we have let a thing like this happen? Did we fail as his parents?

Fast-forward five-plus years, and the definitive answer to that question is *no!* In my heart of hearts, I know we did everything we could've done. Woulda, coulda, and shoulda can go fuck themselves. We couldn't save Rob because Rob didn't want to be saved.

He took his own life, accidentally on purpose, in an impulsive moment, and if it didn't happen then, it would've likely happened in the future. With all his close calls in the past, it was kind of amazing that it hadn't already happened.

I don't think we could've prevented Rob from taking his own life. Nobody could've. He had made up his mind. He was determined. He wanted the pain to stop. He was out of here. His soul knew when it was time to go.

Katarina and I were talking about suicide one night and she told me a story about a man she met who had jumped off the Golden Gate Bridge. He told her that he had regretted it the moment he leaped, like when Wile E. Coyote looks down and realizes that the cliff he's been running on is no longer there. In that split second, the man knew that he wanted to live. He miraculously survived and now helps other people who struggle with what the pros like to call "suicidal ideation."

Rob often leaped without looking, but I don't think he had planned to kill himself that night. Whenever I try to piece it all together, I always come to the same conclusion—that what he did was both opportunistic and impulsive. Shooting yourself with two other people in the room whom you've been drinking and playing video games with all night is just not a premeditated act. To say nothing of leaving behind Biscuit, the cat he had rescued and cared for with all his heart.

We'll never know what he was thinking in that horrible moment when he pulled the trigger, and I'm not saying that he hadn't contemplated taking his own life—I'm pretty sure he had been thinking about it for some time. I'm just suggesting that, like a lot of Rob's plans, this one played out differently than he'd thought.

I've heard that people who are suicidal commonly have blinders on. They can't see past their pain. They can't bear feeling the way they feel. They just want it to stop. They don't think about the people who love them. They don't think about getting help. They don't think that anything can ever change. They see only one way out. Rob—drunk, depressed, desperate—saw an opportunity, grabbed it, and that was that. As Kay Redfield Jamison, perhaps the foremost expert on bipolar disorder, wrote in *Night Falls Fast*, "Suicide . . . is the last and best of bad possibilities."

Unfortunately, there's no going back when you put a gun in your mouth. There's no cliff edge to hang on to, no chance of surviving a fall into San Francisco Bay. It was one and done, which reminds me of another classic Looney Tunes cartoon.

It's the one where Bugs and Daffy perform vaudeville acts, and they're going back and forth, trying to top each other, with Bugs always getting the better of Daffy until we get to the end. Bugs has just finished juggling and the audience is applauding when Daffy runs onstage and says, "I hate you! Now you've forced me to use the act I've held back for a special occasion. Just try and top this one!"

He proceeds to consume nitroglycerin, a goodly amount of gun-powder, and some uranium 238. Then he lights a match—"Girls, you better hold on to your boyfriends!"—and swallows it.

Kaboom! He blows himself up (I remember loving this so much when I was a little kid) and the audience erupts in applause.

"That's terrific, Daffy!" says Bugs. "They want more!"

"I know, I know," says Daffy, who is now a ghost, "but I can only do it once!" And then Daffy rises toward Heaven right before the closing credits music kicks in, accompanied by the famous words, "That's all, folks!"

That's what I imagine Rob saying right before his soul left the building.

· 36 ·

Being and Nothingness

Nothing makes you question your own mortality more than the death of your child. That went double for me because, for as long as I could remember, I had been terrified of the big sleep. I spent countless nights catastrophizing about the end of my days, and whenever my train of thought arrived at the last-stop realization of not being here anymore—the moment I went from being to nothingness—it freaked me out something fierce. It came as a jolt of electricity that nearly stopped my heart.

This amplified death anxiety sprang from my simple certitude that once the light goes out, it's check please, game over, good day sir! I've never been religious and didn't believe in much of anything—until Rob died and changed everything.

I had to believe that Rob's spirit, soul, cosmic energy, or whatever you want to call it exists in some form somewhere. *Not* to believe was simply too painful. My own intense fear of death didn't wholly dissipate until a few years later thanks to several profound psychedelic experiences, which I'll tell you more about soon.

I wouldn't say that I'm necessarily looking forward to my own demise these days—although it will be good to reunite with Rob—but my apprehension about it has been turned down to a low boil. Honestly, I rarely worry about it, mainly since Janie, who is a Buddhist, is fond of reminding me that "Death is certain. It comes without warning. This body will be a corpse." As you can tell, she's a regular Jerry Seinfeld.

When it comes to worrying about my death, Zach has become an excellent proxy. Every time we talk or FaceTime, the first question out of his mouth is "How are you feeling?" What he's really saying is, *Dad, please stay alive!* I understand his concern. He's already suffered one death out of order, and he'd prefer that my turn come many years down the line.

That, unsurprisingly, is also my preference. Even when Rob died, I never thought of not being here. When I was interviewing potential grief therapists, almost every one of them asked if I was suicidal. I thought it was an odd question at first, but then I realized that maybe they thought depression and mental illness ran in our family, because I hadn't yet told them that Rob was adopted. The devastation of losing a child to suicide could also tip someone over the edge, and of course, they didn't know me from Adam. How could they have possibly known that I'm the polar opposite of suicidal? That I'm a cockroach who can survive a hundred nuclear winters!

On the flip side, I've heard many parents in various grief groups over the years comment about how they didn't want to live anymore and they would gladly trade places with their lost child. Some folks said the only reason they are still alive was for the sake of their other kids. Others asserted that there was no reason for them to go on. What was the point? Their child *was* their life. It wasn't that they had a death wish; it was more that they no longer had the will to live.

I know exactly how they felt and so do you. You're so shattered and hopeless in the first weeks and months that you can barely think straight. You truly feel that you don't want to be here anymore. You're the walking dead, barely able to impersonate someone who gives a shit. All signs of life have been sucked out of you.

Those feelings, as you've learned all too well, are completely legit.

Maybe a year down the road—maybe longer, depending on how much or how little work you've put in—a flicker of life returns, taking you by surprise. When this happens (and if it hasn't happened yet, be patient because it will), see if you can hold it in your hands and gently nurture it. As the days go by and the flicker grows into a small flame, a kind of reanimation occurs along with it.

Life looks different to you now. You find yourself acutely aware of the ticking clock, and the moments begin to feel more cherished than ever before. There's no time for bullshit. You're now focused on what really matters. You start to look around for something bigger than yourself, and when you find what that is for you, you go all in and feel alive in a whole new way. You no longer question your own mortality because you've found the answer.

Yes, death is certain. It comes without warning. This body will be a corpse.

But not today.

· 37 ·

Letters from Home

$\mathcal{I}$'ve written countless letters to Rob since he died. Texting was the closest we ever got to writing to each other when he was alive, and that was mainly a one-sided affair in which I tried to talk some sense into him only to be rebuffed by a flurry of emojis that I could never decipher.

In my letters, I told him how I was doing and what he was missing and I'd make a bunch of Dad jokes that I knew would make him wince. I was driven to write these letters because I thought it would be a way to ventilate, because keeping my feelings bottled up inside would stress me out further, and if my thoughts and emotions didn't find an escape hatch, they would remain buried deep inside me, like when I couldn't cry after my mom's death all those years ago. Writing to Rob helped me process what happened to him, what happened to us, and what happened to me.

That's why I'm certain that writing to your child will help you, too. It documents your love and loss, and seeing your feelings come alive on the page connects you with your kid like nothing else.

Staying connected to your child, however, cuts both ways. It opens you up and makes you bleed words of love and pain: sometimes it's sad and beautiful; sometimes it's agonizing and ugly; and sometimes it's all of the above swirled together like a shitty Mister Softee ice cream cone.

In other words, it's just another way of putting in the work. All you have to do is sit down and let the words pour out. Don't think, just write. Tell them how much you love them. Tell them how much you miss them. Tell them the truth about how you're feeling. Tell them whatever you need to tell them.

For example:

Dear Rob,

I know I sent you a letter just a few weeks ago, but I've come to realize how much I like writing to you. It feels slightly less insane than when I'm talking to you out loud. Those convos are incredibly one-sided since you never talk back to me! Which is kind of ironic because that's all you ever did when you were alive. Now you're as quiet as you were when you were a sullen teenager and gave us the silent treatment for days on end. Remember when you used to pull that crap? Good times.

Sometimes I think I'm crazy to speak to you out loud, but mostly I don't. The crazy part may be that I believe you're listening to me. You hardly ever listened to me when you were here, but perhaps that's something that you've learned in being-dead school.

Being dead, what's that like anyway? No joke, I really want to know. What do you do all day? Are there still such things as days or is there some other measurement of time in eternity? When we're young, we think we have all the time in the world. When we're old, we know that we don't. But what about when you're dead and in a whole new spirit world? My guess is that there's no calendar for forever. I just hope that you're keeping busy and staying out of trouble. I know, it's strange that I'm still worrying about you at this late date, but that's a hard habit to break.

I keep thinking how I'll never see you again, at least until I die, which I don't plan on doing anytime soon, so I hope that you don't mind waiting a little bit longer. As much as I love you and want to hang, I'd rather be miserable missing you while staying alive than happy to see you and being dead. It's nothing personal, which also kind of describes your current state of non-being.

It's been six months since you left. Sometimes it feels like yesterday and sometimes it feels like a long time ago and sometimes it feels like it never happened. And that's when it's the absolute worst. Every now and then, just for a few moments, I'll think that you're still here with us, and when that warm bubble suddenly bursts, I get nauseous and feel the shock in my heart. It takes me right back to that terrible Thursday in February, just a few days after Groundhog Day. It's actually a much more disturbing version of *Groundhog Day*. That's what grief is like—only without Bill Murray.

I've been missing you hard this week and I'm not sure why it feels so painful right now. It's been June gloom inside my head for months now. Maybe it's because Maura is in New York and I'm all by myself or maybe it's just that I wish you were still here. I always wish that. And yet I also understand why you did what you did. I really, really do and that makes me even sadder.

I wish there was something that made me feel less sad right now, but that something doesn't exist. That something is you not being dead. Although, full disclosure: there's a good chance that I'd be sad if you *were* still here, just not *as* sad. Neither of us can do anything about that anymore. That time has passed and so have you. You no longer wanted to be here, and it didn't matter what we wanted.

I know I'm not saying anything new here. Sometimes I write in circles just to see where it leads. It might not lead anywhere, but maybe that's where you are. Anywhere, everywhere, and nowhere. Wherever you are sounds like a Beatles song.

I feel like I'm drunk tonight, though I haven't been drinking. You know I'm a lightweight and can't drink more than two of anything. I remember telling you that a while back, and you laughed, but who's laughing now? Trick question! No one is laughing. We haven't laughed for months. You haven't been here to make us laugh, and you *not* being here has only made us cry.

And that often makes me angry. I got angry at you plenty when you were alive, but now that you're gone, I can't stay angry at you for very long. I know I've said it before, but I'll say it again—I just miss you so damn much. Every day. Every hour. Every minute. Every second. Now and forever.

Right before I go to bed, I look at the photo of you that's on the bedroom wall and remember when you were a little boy. Those are some of my best memories of you. I'd read you a bedtime story, give you a kiss, and tuck you in for the night. "Goodnight, Rob," I'd say, just like I've been saying out loud every night since you died. And just like you did, I close my eyes and fall asleep.

In my dreams, we're always together.

Love,
Dad

• 38 •

Face Time

$\mathcal{B}$uddhists call it "walking through the fire." Therapists refer to it as "when things get messy." I've talked about "facing the grief beast." It's all different ways of saying the same thing: at some point, you have to look at what scares you the most and begin to move through it.

I can't tell you when—only you know when—but I can tell you how.

With apologies to Nike: just do it!

I don't mean to make light of anything you've been avoiding. I'm sure you've been avoiding it for a very good reason—you're scared. You're scared that looking at it will hurt more than anything has ever hurt. You're scared that you'll never get past it and be eternally stuck in this circle of grief.

I was scared too. We're all scared. How can you not be? This confrontation has been a long time coming and will be one of the hardest things you'll ever do.

The good news is—you've already been doing it.

You've been taking small steps forward for several months now. You've been breaking down your monumental loss into bite-size pieces that no longer engulf you. You've asked and answered every question that has been torturing you. You've been processing and integrating your loss into your daily life without even knowing it.

You're tougher than you think you are. You're ready. You've got this!

Now it's time to listen to your heart. Your heart is no longer scared of anything. Your heart is fearless. Your heart has been busy repairing itself, right under your nose, while you've been putting in the work.

133

Your heart is filled with the love of your child and is prepared to take on all comers.

Which is not to say that you won't still hurt. You will, but you're no longer afraid of feeling the terrible sting of sorrow. In a strange way, you almost welcome it because you've discovered that the pain can help you heal. The pain gives you strength, like flame hardens steel. You're about to move through the fire with determination and grace.

It feels easier to endure, and the longer you stay in there facing what scares you the most, the faster you'll move toward the light at the end of the grief tunnel. This is the great leap you've been waiting for or has been thrust upon you, and once you take it, there's no turning back.

You're not completely out of the woods yet, and some days will still suck because that's just the way it is and will be. But things are different now because you are different now.

I made several leaps after Rob's death, starting with the recognition and acceptance of his mental illness. I had a much harder time with my second big jump—getting a grip on exactly what happened on the night he shot himself.

Every time I tried to picture Rob holding a gun to his head, I felt sick, and I'd deflect that nightmare image with a flood of questions: How did he get a gun? Who were the people in his apartment? What was his state of mind that night? How do we know it was definitely suicide? How could he have done this to us?

These questions continued to swirl around in my head for almost a year until one of my last sessions with Katarina. She asked me to visualize the night Rob killed himself. She felt that I needed to take a close look at the most traumatic moment that changed all of our lives. She insisted that it had become an anchor that was weighing me down and that I needed to cut the rope attached to it and sail off into the rest of my life.

I resisted at first, which immediately told me this was something I had to finally contend with. And that's when my heart decided to take over.

I closed my eyes and saw Rob sitting on his beat-up leather couch, drunk on malt liquor, petting his cat Biscuit. He looked so sad and so alone. He took a pull on the forty and threw the can across the living room. He picked up a gun that he had stashed under one of the leather cushions and started to play with it. Twirling it around and pointing it at the window that looked out at the ocean, he made soft "pew pew" gun sounds and then blew on the tip of the barrel, just like he did when he was a little boy playing with his first toy gun.

His friends were in the bedroom doing who knows what. He slipped in a pair of Apple AirPods, cranked up "New Crack" by Wax, his go-to song to rap to, and slowly raised the gun to his head. He paused for just a moment and so did I. That moment, I imagined, felt like a lifetime to both of us.

"Fuck it. Peace out," he finally whispered and pulled the trigger.

The next thing I saw was Rob looking incredibly surprised when he got to the other side. "Dang! What the hell just happened?" I imagined him saying, and then I opened my eyes.

I went through an entire box of tissues that night, and before I got up to leave, Katarina said one last invaluable thing.

"Give yourself permission to be," she urged.

And from that day on, I did.

• 39 •

Long Ago and Faraway

You know the famous aversion therapy scene from *A Clockwork Orange* when they stretch Malcolm McDowell's eyelids wide open with a pair of clamps and force him to watch ultraviolent images? That's what I thought of when I sat down on the couch to watch home videos of Rob a week or so before the unveiling of his headstone. I chose not to play Beethoven's Ninth.

The last time I had watched these blasts from the past was a few days after Rob died, when we were all miserably hanging out at Caryn's house in Long Island. I remember how we were crying and laughing at the same time, which isn't that easy to do, and finally had to shut it off because we just couldn't take it anymore. As I braced myself for another viewing, I wasn't sure why I was about to put myself through this time-travel torture again, but now I know that it was nothing more than my last great leap.

I popped in the first DVD (I had digitized our old videotapes a few years back), poured a glass of Syrah, and pressed play. I was fully prepared to enter Guinness World Records as the world's tallest puddle of tears.

Watching our old life flash before my eyes almost a year later was different right from the start. The first thing up was Robbie (it was always Robbie and Zachy when they were little) in one of those baby walkers that look like a car with a tiny steering wheel. He was talking gibberish a mile a minute, which was just under the speed limit. Five seconds later, he began to scream bloody murder.

"He's sad because he just learned that he's a Jew!" I said.

I found myself laughing at this little joke, which took me by surprise.

I fast-forwarded every few seconds because, let's face it, watching hours of any baby—even the cutest infant in the world, which Rob most definitely was—doing plenty of nothing is boring as hell. I stopped on Caryn bathing him in the sink. According to the time stamp, he was three months old.

"This is what Robbie loves the best," she cooed. "He loves his baths!"

"And . . . " I prodded.

"And what?"

"And he loves his Daddy!" I said, right before the little bastard shot a stream of pee at me. That was the beginning of Rob's sense of humor.

More fast-forwarding and there was Robbie eating plastic keys and I said, "He'll love to see this twenty years from now!" Which, luckily, he got to do when he came to visit me in Park Slope a few years before officially moving to California. He couldn't believe that he was once so little, the same way I can't believe that he's no longer with us.

I put in another DVD titled "Robbie's Next Six Months," and it began with Caryn reading him *Pat the Bunny*. Robbie seemed to really like it and soon began chewing on his new favorite book. He was a little cranky this day, teetering on the verge of tears, but mainly he sounded like he was trying to tell us something very important.

"Who is he talking to all the time?" Caryn asked. "The aliens!" I said as he started to munch on his foot.

Next up was Robbie eating baby food for the first time and washing it down with a few hits from his ba-ba. My in-laws, Marty and Phyllis, were there, as they often were in those early days, and after feeding Robbie a few more spoonfuls, Caryn asked, "Is he the cutest thing you've ever seen?"

"Yes," I answered softly from my couch as I took a long sip of wine.

Music was always playing in our house back then, and Robbie had impeccable taste right from the get-go. He seemed to like Dylan's version of "This Old Man," but he really smiled hard when Caryn danced around with him to "Itsy Bitsy Spider." God, how we loved that little boy! A few more fast-forwards and splish, splash, we were takin' a bath with special guest Marty singing "Mother and Child Reunion." It made me happy to think that they were now back together again.

I loaded in another DVD labeled "More Stuff," which started with Robbie sticking out his tongue again and again as if he were licking an imaginary ice cream cone. Caryn was cracking up, and then Marty picked him up and rubbed Robbie's little belly on his bald head, and Robbie was giggling, and we were all laughing, and there I was sitting on the couch with a big smile on my face as I remembered this sweet, sweet time in our life.

The biggest surprise of all was that I cried only three times, all triggered by music. The first time was watching Robbie at five months old, zipping around in his walker while holding a Mylar balloon for Caryn's birthday. James Taylor was singing "You've Got a Friend," and you'd have to be made of stone not to blubber while hearing "Winter, spring, summer, or fall, all you have to do is call . . ."

The second time was when the kids were four or five (there was no date stamp) and dancing around maniacally to Vince Guaraldi's "Christmas Time Is Here" while playing with our new wheaten terrier puppy, Mookie. Robbie chased Mookie all around the living room until they finally plopped down on the floor together. Zachy, for reasons unknown, ran over and started to rub Robbie's head.

"I'm messing up his hair," Zachy said, and the three of us were hysterically laughing. To top it off, Zachy danced over to the camera and blew a kiss, which just got me into Guinness World Records.

The third time was watching a video of Zachy singing and dancing to "Wonderwall," a Carlat family favorite. It's just about the cutest and happiest thing I've ever seen, and I didn't realize how bad I needed to see it again. I didn't realize how bad I needed to see all of this, and just how good it would make me feel. I needed a reminder that, long ago and far away, our life was beautiful.

I watched that Zachy video over and over again (Robbie makes a special guest appearance at the very end) and cried for joy each time. It was the first time in a long time that I had cried for that reason.

For at least one night, to paraphrase Malcolm McDowell's Alex, I was cured.

· *40* ·

Signs of Love

*Y*our child is well onto their next journey, but they're still here, there, and everywhere. All you have to do is look.

Your child is in the book you're reading. Your child is on every other TV show you're watching. Your child is in the bite of pizza you're eating. Your child is in every song you listen to. Your child is in the marigolds sitting on your desk. Your child is staring back at you in the mirror.

Your child is with you when you're shopping at Ralphs and inadvertently toss their favorite backyard barbecue potato chips into your cart. Your child is with you when you're folding laundry and get to the Steely Dan T-shirt they bought you for Father's Day many years ago. Your child is with you when you hit the vape pen late at night and reflect on how much you miss them.

Your child is always with you because you carry your child in your heart.

Sometimes these memories make you smile, sometimes they make you cry, sometimes they make you drunk with love, and sometimes they make you feel empty inside, but they keep you connected to your child, and that's all that really matters.

Not a day goes by without something you do or watch or read or taste or smell reminding you of your child, and that's in addition to all the signs they leave to show they've come to visit. Who knew that the powers that be keep them so busy on the other side? My friend Robert, whose son Walker shot himself a few years back, sees ravens. The day after Walker died, a raven swooped down and landed in his backyard. It has since returned with a flock, sometimes doing a flyby just a few feet over his head, as if to say, "Hi Dad! It's me! Wut up?"

The signs are different for all of us, but one thing they have in common is that they're all signs of love. I mentioned that Fleur the psychic medium told me to look for feathers and for Caryn to keep an eye out for sunflowers. For the first year after Rob died, Caryn saw sunflowers wherever she looked, but I didn't see a single feather. I remember joking, "WTF! The lazy bum can only do one or the other?"

He finally got around to hitting me up with feathers, and every time I see one now, I point to it and say, "Hi Rob!" or "Dude!" The feathers are really a perfect choice. It feels like he's tickling me to make me laugh, which is just so Rob. I was happy to make his job easier last year, when I moved in with Janie at the beach, where there's plumage galore.

When Rob's not dropping in with feathers, I tune in to watch him on TV. He's on two of my favorite shows (that I know he would've loved): *Reservation Dogs* and *The Bear*, which, not coincidentally, are about suicide and grief, among many things. If you haven't watched them, check them out because they're brilliant and funny, but also—spoiler alert!—absolutely heartbreaking.

There were two brief moments in their respective season finales that floored me. At the end of season two, the Rez Dog kids walk into the Pacific Ocean and hug each other, and the spirit of Daniel—their friend who killed himself—suddenly appears beside them, joining the group hug. At the end of *The Bear*'s first season, the very last shot is of the great actor Jon Bernthal, who plays Mikey—and who also killed himself—smiling hard at his younger brother, Carmy. It will come as no surprise that all I saw was Rob.

Our kids are also fond of visiting us in our dreams, and Rob is no exception, although he comes infrequently. At first, I thought that he was just occupied with his booming feather business, until my friend Sarah texted me about a dream she recently had in which Rob appeared. Just like him to show up in somebody else's dreams!

Whenever he deigns to drop in to one of mine, he appears only as Little Robbie, and I'm not sure why, other than that was when he was most adorable. I could barely remember any of these dreams, except for the following one that I had the wherewithal to write down.

I'm walking on Venice Beach right before sunset, and aside from a few rowdy homeless guys and the steady beat of the drum circle, it is beautiful and peaceful and—of course and appropriately—smells like weed. I watch the waves gently breaking on the shore, and it feels hypnotic, so I close my eyes for a few seconds. When I open them, I see a small sailboat on the horizon. As it comes into view, it looks like the one from Where the Wild Things Are, *but instead of Max in his wolf costume, it's Robbie in his G.I. Joe pajamas. He sails a little closer to shore and we both start frantically waving to each other, and he's yelling something, but I can't hear what it is because the drums are getting faster and louder. And then the bow of the sailboat slowly turns around and heads out to the open sea, and that's when my heart tells me what he was saying. Robbie is still waving and I'm standing on the shore waving back, and he keeps sailing farther and farther away until he is just a speck. Then, all of a sudden, he's gone.*

· *41* ·

Comic Relief

$\mathcal{W}$hoever said "Tragedy plus time equals comedy" seriously miscalculated for those of us who have lost a child. We're a perennially tough crowd, and it takes a lot just to get a smile out of us, which, more often than not, is fake.

It's hard to laugh when you're miserable, but sometimes after a rough patch, when we're exhausted and all cried out, we're desperate for relief, comic or otherwise. I can't think of a group of people who need to laugh more than we do! Humor is a way we deal with the pain of life, and what's more painful than death?

Yet we tend to deny ourselves this respite from our daily dread, particularly in the early, unfunniest days, when we wake up with what I like to call "mourning breath." Even if you think something is funny (like that silly pun), it feels almost sacrilegious to laugh when you're feeling as torn up as we feel. We don't allow ourselves to lose our shit because we've already lost so much.

We feel guilty about laughing. We say it's inappropriate or disrespectful. It's "too soon." But really, it's not. Actually, it can't happen soon enough. The most therapeutic thing we can do for ourselves is laugh.

Laughing helps us cope. Laughing reduces stress, tension, and anxiety. Laughter eases fear and anger. Laughter helps us tolerate pain. Laughter produces a sense of control, joy, and hope. Laughter shifts our perspective and brings us back to life. Laughter helps us heal.

So why aren't we laughing our asses off? Why aren't we turning grim into grin? If laughter is the best medicine, why aren't we all heavily medicated with glee?

I like to blame it on our so-called life. We often get wrapped up in our own grief entanglements and can easily go a day, a week, or even longer without laughter. We're in the dark for what feels like forever before we can see the first rays of light. There's not a whole lot of laughing in the darkness, unless you can go back in time to a movie theater and see Mel Brooks or Steve Martin when they were in their prime.

We need to laugh just like we need to go to the gym and stay in shape. We need to exercise our funny bone every day. I know it sounds a little weird, reminding you to laugh, but there are worse things to be reminded of, and I don't need to remind you of those worse things.

If you have to, schedule some time for mirth in your calendar:

11:00–11:30 a.m.: Watch cats stuck in the toilet memes and singing dog videos on TikTok.
3:30–4:00 p.m.: Check out Steve Carell's best bloopers from *The Office*.

I asked Zach what his go-tos are when it comes to a quick comedy fix, and without hesitation he said, "Funny game show answers!" and proceeded to share this *Family Feud* gem with me:

QUESTION: Name a yellow fruit.

ANSWER: Orange.

My go-tos that always crack me up are clips from *Monty Python and the Holy Grail*. It was one of Rob's favorite movies, and we watched it together countless times. Whenever I'm feeling a little funky, I'm happy to slide down into that hilarious rabbit hole, which includes the killer bunny who viciously bloodies any of King Arthur's knights who approach the cave it's protecting.

Our two most beloved scenes were "The Black Knight" (*Tis but a scratch!*) and "Bring out Your Dead!" (*I'm not dead!*). If you're not familiar with this comedy classic, check it out on YouTube, as clips from the movie stand on their own. Every time I watch them, I can hear Rob's laugh, and that instantly puts a big smile on my face.

· *42* ·

The Presence of Their Absence

There were days when I just missed Rob so damn much that I could barely stand it. It came out of nowhere, triggered by nothing, and I found myself overwhelmed by the presence of his absence.

His silence was deafening, and all I wanted to do was cry.

Sometimes I felt the presence of his absence when I talked with Caryn or Zach. Sometimes it was when someone asked if I had any kids. Sometimes I'd look up at the sky and almost see Rob hiding behind a cloud. Sometimes it was nothing more than hearing a distant whisper in the middle of the night and sometimes the sound was piercing, like on his birthday. Sometimes the presence of Rob's absence felt worse than the absence of his presence.

I'm sure you've had strange days like these too. You may wake up early in the morning when it's nice and quiet, longing to hear your child's voice again. You may be driving somewhere, and the vacant shotgun seat suddenly fills you with sorrow. You may hug yourself before you go to sleep at night, wishing you could wrap your arms around your baby one more time. There's nothing in this world that feels lonelier than the presence of your child's absence, and it takes time before you can do anything about it.

It's a crushing blow, and my main advice will come as no surprise because it's pretty much the same advice I've been giving you throughout this book—let yourself tumble into the abyss, lean into whatever you're feeling, and allow those emotions to work their magic.

Feeling the depth of your loss—rolling around in it at the bottom of the bottom until it seeps into your bones and begins to transform you—is yet another way of facing what scares you the most.

That being said, you don't necessarily need to spend the *whole* day being haunted by your child's absence. Whenever I felt trapped in the bottomless pit of Rob's nonexistence, I took the initial hit and then tried to dig myself out by changing the narrative. I tapped into a happy memory and hoped that it would take hold. Sometimes it worked, sometimes it didn't, but there was nothing to lose by shining a light in the darkness.

My happy memories with Rob were sporadic, which is why I always travel back in time to a Christmas past, weeks before Rob killed himself. Zach had flown in from Tampa and the three of us had a blast. We had taken Rob to his first-ever basketball game, and it felt like a weekend from long ago when Caryn was at work and it was just the boys. On Christmas Day, Rob and Zach busted each other's balls like only brothers can, and we all gleefully stuffed our faces. It was a magnificent day that later turned bittersweet, because it was the last time the three of us were together. Yet I'm eternally grateful that Rob gave us this beautiful parting gift.

Making the choice to turn on the guiding light and climb out of the hole was another great leap forward. I remember having this epiphany—that I can choose how I want to coexist with my grief—about a year after Rob died. The notion that I didn't have to suffer in order to maintain a loving connection with him, that I could let go of the pain without letting go of Rob, was a revelation.

I was in so much agony for such a long time that I couldn't see straight. I couldn't see what was right in front of me because my tears got in the way. Understanding that I had agency in determining how I wanted to move forward with my mourning felt like some kind of miracle. Recognizing that you can choose how to proceed is perhaps the most significant turning point toward beginning the next chapter of your life and becoming an extraordinary parent.

We'll talk more about the importance of choice shortly, but I'd like to get back to the presence/absence thing for a moment. Now that Rob's been gone for some time, I feel only his presence. I carry him with me wherever I go. I keep him close. I talk to him. I laugh with him. I cry with him. Rob is neither present nor absent. Rob is always.

· 43 ·

O-o-h Child,
Things Are Gonna Get Easier

Whether you're ready for it or not, the pain of losing a child eases over time. It just does. Its grip becomes less. It's still pain, and when it does pay a visit, it still throbs, but it's not as intense as it was in the early dark days. Pain is no longer your constant companion.

Things are gonna get easier. As the months (and in some cases, years) go by, you're no longer crying every day. You're out and about in the world as a semi-functioning human being. The fog of grief is slowly lifting, and you can see clearly again. The spark of life is gradually returning to your eyes.

This is a good thing, although there's a good chance that it doesn't feel good. How could it? Nothing can ever bring your child back, and yet, little by little, you're learning to cope with and accept the reality of your loss. Reality still bites, but it no longer draws blood, and at the same time, the prospect of your own happiness has floated its way back into the picture.

You're actually surprised that you feel this way, because for the longest time this wasn't even an option. You didn't care about the rest of your life because you felt that your life was over, just like it is for your child. When you look back on the early days of your grief and compare it to how you feel a year later, it's truly amazing how far you've come. You still have a way to go, but you're getting there.

You've taken positive steps and made great leaps forward. You've reconciled with many of the things that have been troubling you as well as the things you inflicted upon yourself. You've put in the work and faced what scared you the most. You're now a fearless warrior who has mastered walking through fire.

149

Essentially, two things have happened that have been game chang-
ers. The first was realizing that you now have a choice in how to move
forward. (Reminder: when it comes to grief, you don't move on, you
move forward.) You are no longer on autopilot. You're in control,
maybe for the first time since your child's death. Where you go and
what you'll do from here is completely in your own hands.

The second thing is an unexpected reward for taking control of
your life, the reemergence of one of my favorite four-letter words—
hope! Hope, if you recall, is the light at the end of the grief tunnel. Hope
makes you look forward to the next day. Hope heals your heart. As Rob
would say, "Hope is dope!"

And once it returns, it's there for keeps. You can never lose hope
again because you've worked so hard to get it back. Take that in for a
moment and, while you're at it, give yourself some props for enduring
what most people think is unendurable. What those people don't know
is that you didn't really have any choice. But that in no way diminishes
your remarkable journey of survival and recovery.

Okay, so that's the good news, and there really isn't any bad news
when you've reached the other side of the grief tunnel. However, I'm
not suggesting that it's all beautiful memory rainbows and sweet "missing you" lollipops from here on out. You will still hurt, you will still
sob, and there will still be days when you miss your kid something awful.
But you'll be able to handle the pain in a way that you weren't able to
before. You'll let it wash over you and then you'll dry your tears, eat
dinner, watch some TV, and get a good night's sleep. The pain will no
longer linger because you won't allow it to.

The pain is just a reminder of how much you loved your child.

The next part of your grief journey awaits. and, compared to what
you've already been through, it's a piece of cake (very likely angel food).
It focuses on accepting the reality of your loss and choosing a kind of
happiness that allows the light to coexist with the dark. It's about maintaining an enduring connection with your child while relearning what
it means to live a full and meaningful life. It's about coming out of the
other side of hell transformed. It's about becoming extraordinary.

· 44 ·

What to Expect When You're Expecting to Cry Forever

$\mathscr{I}$ didn't know where to turn for help right after Rob died, so I did what we all do nowadays and searched the internet. I don't even remember what I was looking for exactly, probably just something that would take away a tiny bit of pain or provide some semblance of an explanation or the slightest ray of hope.

Try googling "parents who have lost a child to suicide" . . . um, on second thought, maybe don't. After that fruitless search thoroughly bummed me out, I came across a handout from my initial intake meeting at Our House entitled "Grief Is a Process." When I first read it, I thought it was generic fluff, an obvious and optimistic roadmap kind of thing that you might find in the waiting room of a therapist's office.

The truth was that it was impossible for me to process anything at the time, least of all grief. I was a dead man walking and could barely read through my tears. Everything felt so empty and meaningless, especially words.

But now that Rob's been gone for more than a few years, I thought it might be time to revisit the words in that grief guide and add some 20/20 hindsight of my own.

Grief Is a Process
A better title would be "What to Expect When You're Expecting to Cry Forever."
Here are some realistic expectations for your grief as time goes by.

Maybe the first thing they should have said here is: "You can't possibly comprehend what you're about to read, so just give it a quick scan, then put it away and come back to it a year from now."

It takes time for healing to happen. Although the pain of grief often comes upon us all at once in a crushing blow, the pain gradually lessens over time.

The pain and crushing parts are certainly true, and both abate eventually. But I'd tweak the first sentence to read: "It takes a lifetime for healing to happen, but you need to work at it, because it doesn't happen all by itself."

You will find relief through expressing your feelings even many months and years after the death of your loved one.

So here's the thing about relief: on a micro level, sure, there's some solace in letting out your feelings rather than keeping them bottled up inside. But on a macro level, I don't feel especially relieved. Sure, maybe there's a respite from the pain, but there's no relief when it comes to missing Rob. There's no relief from the absence of someone you loved.

You cannot get through this alone, so find ways to seek out support.

Seeing a therapist, joining a grief group, and talking about Rob with family and close friends were all incredibly helpful, and I couldn't imagine enduring this without that wonderful support. But ultimately, we all go through grief on our own and come out from the other side a changed person.

The camaraderie and understanding of others in a grief support group will help to normalize your feelings.

I never imagined myself in a grief group. I'm pretty uncomfortable in just about any group setting, so I couldn't see myself being any different with a bunch of strangers whom I had absolutely nothing in common with other than that we had all recently suffered the worst thing that could ever happen to a parent. Yet the moment I walked into my first meeting, I knew I was with my people. We all spoke the same language, and the only place we truly felt understood was in that room.

It helps to continue to honor and maintain a loving connection to the memory of the person who died.

Writing about Rob helped me stay connected to him like nothing else. For the first few months, I was compelled to document how I was feeling and dealing with his loss as well as how those feelings might change over the course of time. But as the years have gone by, I've become more aware of the "loving connection to the memory" part.

In other words, focusing on Rob's true self rather than just recounting all the bad craziness he got himself into. So good call, "Grief Is a Process" guide!

There will come a time when you will go for an hour, a day or a week without crying.

I didn't believe this could be possible when I first read it, but of course it's true. We can't cry endlessly. And the biggest revelation happened years later, when a passing thought about Rob had me crying for joy.

You will be able to talk about your loved one without feeling an overwhelming sadness.

As I'm sure you've figured out by now, the takeaway with almost all of these milestones is that, in the early days of grief, you just can't imagine that anything will ever change, and certainly not for the better. It does and it can.

You find yourself laughing or enjoying yourself.

Amazingly, yes and yes.

You are able to smile as you think of tender memories.

It took some time, but right again, Grief Process Guide!

You find yourself wanting to spend time with others.

Well, let's not get too crazy here!

You begin to see and feel a possibility of hope for a meaningful life ahead.

So how does it feel to be mostly right about everything, Mr. Grief Is a Process know-it-all?

Me and You, Part 2

$\mathcal{T}$he middle was the hardest part. Once you get through it, it's all up-hill from there. There's still work to be done, but it's a different type of work that concentrates more on what comes next and less on what has taken place. Before we get to all of that good stuff, however, it's time for another check-in.

ME: So, it's been a minute. How're you doing, my friend?

YOU: Better. Worse. I don't know.

ME: That sounds about right.

YOU: Some days I'm depressed. Some days I'm busy and distracted. Some days I'm living in the past. Some days I'm present in the moment. Any way you look at it, I still don't feel like I'm the one doing the choosing, but I push through because there's no other choice.

ME: It may not feel like it, but you're choosing life. You're choosing to get out of bed every morning and live in the real world. "Pushing through" is an interesting choice of words. It almost sounds like giving birth.

YOU: Ugh! I never want to do that again.

ME: I don't blame you, but it's really more about *your* rebirth—beginning a new life without your child.

YOU: That makes me sad, but I get what you're saying.

ME: What I'm really saying is that you no longer need to be connected to the pain in order to stay connected to your child. Speaking of which, has any aspect of grief become easier?

YOU: Well, I'm no longer in unrelenting agony. I'm no longer free-falling in the pit of despair. The initial devastation has worn off, but that doesn't mean that I'm now shiny, happy people. So are things easier? Well, if you compare it to a heart attack, then I would say yes.

ME: What about you? How've you changed? What's different about you since your child died?

YOU: I'm not sure. I know I've been, as you like to say, "putting in the work" and taking steps forward, and I've even faced a few of the things that scared me the most. I'm in a grief group and I see a therapist once a week, and both have been extremely helpful. I talk to my kid every day and I really like the way that feels. I don't beat myself up as much. Still, I can't really tell you that I've changed.

ME: Actually, you just did!

YOU: I guess, maybe. . . . I just never feel happy, you know? There's always a dark cloud overhead. Sometimes a ray of light peeks through, but it doesn't last very long.

ME: Give it time, and it will. A transformation is taking place that's difficult for you to see right now.

YOU: That may be true, but I'll never be the same. Things will never be the same. My heart is broken and beyond repair.

ME: You'd be surprised. Your heart, as you'll recall if you've ever seen *Hannah and Her Sisters*, is a very, very resilient muscle. And it's the strongest hearts that have the most scars. Your heart has been guiding you through the thickets of grief and has never steered you wrong. Keep listening to your heart.

YOU: The thing that hurts my heart the most, the thing that I can't make peace with, the thing that haunts me more than anything is how much I miss my child. The more time that goes by, the more I miss him, and I can't imagine that ever changing.

ME: Missing him doesn't change, but your relationship with your child does. When I think about Rob these days, I know he's at peace, that he's doing well wherever he is, and that provides incredible comfort. When we talk, I know I'm talking to his true spirit, and it's as close to a heart-to-heart as any conversation we ever had.

YOU: But how do you know he's at peace? How do you know there's something else after we shuffle off this mortal coil?

ME: I know because that's what I choose to believe. I choose to believe Rob's spirit exists in some version of *The Good Place*. I choose to believe that psychic mediums have contacted him and that he's spoken to me through them. And even more woo-woo than that, I choose to believe that Rob's spirit is magnificent because I've seen it with my own eyes during several psychedelic trips.

YOU: Wait! What?

ME: I'll tell you more about that a little later on. But so much of healing is determined by the choices we make. What choices have you made to help yourself?

YOU: Funny you ask. We just had the one-year anniversary of our son's death, and my husband and I decided to dedicate the next year to reengaging with the world. We're going to take better care of ourselves and really get back to enjoying our lives. We know that's what our son would want us to do.

ME: That's fantastic! Congratulations!

YOU: Well, that lasted for about two weeks, and then we were both back in Funkytown. And we've remained there ever since.

ME: I know exactly what you mean, because the same thing happened to me. I was trying too hard. I was trying not to feel what I was feeling. I was trying to trick myself into thinking that I was ready while also trying to outmaneuver grief.

YOU: So now what do we do?

ME: Your intentions were 100 percent on the money. It sounds like your timing was off. You'll know when the time is right because you knew that the previous timing was wrong.

YOU: Above all else, I really hope we can find happiness in our life again.

ME: I have no doubt you will. You've already made that choice. Listen to your heart and I can assure you it'll happen.

YOU: I'm going to hold you to that.

ME: I'm happy to be held.

YOU: I keep thinking about what's ahead and how we want to live our lives, and I'm struggling with those answers right now. I feel like we not only need to honor our son by enjoying ourselves, but more than ever before, I have this real need to do something meaningful with my life.

ME: I'm so glad you said that! It's just a perfect transition to part III— The Beginning

Part III

THE BEGINNING

· *46* ·

Never Let Me Go

$\mathcal{R}$ight now you might not feel like you're at the beginning of anything, much less the beginning of the rest of your life. It's not like we can completely start over and pretend that what has happened never happened. We can't alter the past, but we can change how we choose to move forward.

Don't worry, your grief isn't going anywhere. Little by little, you'll learn to absorb it until you forget that it was once a separate entity that scared the shit out of you. You've been moving through it at your own speed while putting in the work, and at some point down the road, you'll wake up and decide it's finally time to let go. Just to reassure you, you're not letting go of your child. You're letting go of the pain and suffering and fully accepting the reality of losing them.

Letting go is scary. What if you lose your connection with your kid and no longer miss them? What if it feels like you've abandoned them? What if you feel guilty for *not* feeling sad? What if you fall so far into the grief abyss now that you have nothing to grasp?

What actually happens is the opposite of everything you feared. Once you're able to let go of the agonizing thoughts that you've clung to since the day you got the terrible news, you'll feel stronger—no, it's more than that, you'll feel, for the first time in a long time, a sense of freedom and control, which sounds contradictory but no less mindblowing. Most of all, you'll feel a different and deeper connection with your child.

Strangely, I had a more difficult time letting go of Rob while he was still among us. I was never able to just sit back and wait for him to "bottom out" and that went double for "Let go, let God" or doing the "detach with love" thing. It all made perfect sense in my head. My head was never the problem. Tough love just never felt right to me—and yes, I was well aware that was the way it was supposed to feel, but I didn't care. And neither did my heart.

It was my heart that eventually helped me let go of Rob, but my memory is fuzzy other than it seemed to have crept up on me. I don't remember the exact time and place when I let go, because I don't think there was an exact time and place. It was gradual and imperceptible, similar to the way we change while processing our grief.

Observing it from a distance now, it looks as though one day I was a heartbroken sad sack that could barely lace up his sneakers and the next day I was walking barefoot on the beach with Janie making plans for dinner. Somewhere between those two days, I let go of the pain in the ass that was Rob in life—as well as the pain in my heart set off by his death. Letting go is just another aspect of grief that you can't possibly recognize while you're tumbling around inside the belly of the beast.

It was my heart, about a year after Rob died, that also helped me simplify my life by choosing to live in the moment. I no longer looked back because other than learning from the past (which all of us have endured and then some), it just seemed hollow and pointless.

I also stopped future tripping because I had learned—in the hardest way possible—that things tend to unfold in ways that I never could have imagined. Future tripping only triggered feelings of anxiety, which I already had more than my fair share of.

How I managed to stop was surprisingly simple. I remember meditating for a short while (for whatever reason, that practice never stuck) and repeating the words, "This is the only moment," and since then, I've been more present and have felt more alive than ever before.

This para-Buddhist outlook also informs how I view Rob today. I haven't and will never let go of him, as you'll never let go of your child, but I have reworked the way I remember him.

I've let go of all of his bullshit that drove me crazy. I've let go of the near–heart attacks I had whenever I saw his name pop up on my iPhone. I've let go of being scared of what Rob might do to us, what he might do to someone else, but mostly what he might do to himself. I've let go of the version of Rob who made our past tense.

At the same time, I've let go of Rob's future. I've let go of him calling one day with good news. I've let go of seeing him take a five-year chip at an AA meeting. I've let go of the fantasy that Rob finally would get his shit together, find a good woman, have a bunch of kids, settle down, and live happily ever after. I've let go of us growing old together.

When I think about Rob today, it's never about the past or the future. It's about how I feel about him at this very moment. How much I love him and how much I adore all the good that was inside him. That's the way I choose to remember him. The best of Rob is all that's left, and that's what I hold most dear.

• 47 •

The Son Also Rises

⌘

Yo,

I know you've already heard a lot about me, so I asked my dad if I could talk to you guys directly . . . because somebody has to call him out on his half-baked ideas and stupid advice! Hahaha, I'm just playing with you! My dad's a straight shooter . . . and so was I. Hope that didn't *trigger* anybody.

Sorry, I couldn't resist. It's bad enough that there's no cursing here, but at least the Big Man lets us keep our sense of humor.

I really do have a few things to say to you, but it's not just me saying them. I'm actually representing all of your sons and daughters because I'm the lucky one with a dad writing a book about all this dead kid stuff.

So, what do your kids want you to know? I made a list but can't find it, so I'm just gonna wing it, and no, I'm not an angel and neither are your children. Okay, first of all, we're all hanging out on this side together, just chillin' all peaceful-like. Nobody's in pain and everybody gets along great because that's the way things work in the spirit world. We left all of our baggage on Earth and only took the very best of who we were with us, and that's the God's honest truth, which is as much as I can tell you because otherwise He gets super pissed.

Second, your kids want you to know there was nothing you could've done to prevent them from ending up here. Whatever they were suffering from or whatever terrible, random thing happened to them was supposed to happen. Our time was up and now we're working on what comes next. Don't beat yourselves up about any of it. For real. We know you did your best.

You know we can see and hear you, right? I can't explain how (there are so many crazy rules on this side!) but just know that we're always watching and listening. It's like you guys have become our new favorite TV show.

And that's how we know you've been having a hard time ever since we split. We hate to see you suffering and want you to *please, please, please*, stop worrying about us! There's nothing to worry about anymore. We're all good and we want you to be too! Honestly, we're worried about *you!* We worry about you getting stuck in your sadness, so maybe stop looking at our baby pictures and videos so much! We know that we were adorable, but it's not gonna bring any of us back or make you feel any better. Unless it does and, in that case, have at it!

We get the heavy sadness thing a thousand percent and know you're going to do whatever feels right for you, but we also want you to *get on with your life!* We know we're the only ones who could say that without making you angry, which is why we just did. We understand it's hard to live without us (just like it was hard to live with some of us, and that includes yours truly), but you really don't have any other choice. And do us all a big favor—delete our names and numbers from your cell phones already! We can't call you back!

We miss you and wish we could still be there with you. But here's a little secret—sometimes we are! You can't see us, but we know you can sometimes feel our presence. That little pang, or whatever it's called, that you sometimes feel in your heart? That's us! Hello! We're right there! We're right where we've always been and will always be.

The only unpleasant thing about crossing over is seeing all of you guys hurting so much, and that's why my dad wants you to read this letter whenever you're feeling all the feels. We love you with all of our hearts and know you feel the same way about us, and that's the most important thing in the world. Your world and ours.

In the meantime, we want you guys to stop being soooooo sad and think about all the other beautiful things in your life. Stop wasting your energy on tormenting yourselves. We know you need to grieve but enough with the weepy stuff already! And maybe listen to some of the things my dad's been suggesting. He also wanted me to tell you that maybe you should try writing a letter *from* your kid. It gives us a chance to spend some quality time together and makes our absence a little more present. (I don't know about you, but I still don't understand that whole "presence of your absence, absence of your presence" thing my dad was talking about.)

Bottom line: grief is forever, but that doesn't mean you have to continue to suffer. You've suffered enough. You all have. So enough with the suffering, too! Go out and eat a giant pizza cake or cake pizza like we have here! (Dad, you'd love them!)

You were all great dads, moms, brothers, sisters, and friends. Maybe we could've been better people, or maybe not, but at the end of the day, we were just who we were. The one big thing we've learned since you last saw us is that we'll do better next time. We've learned a lot in our lives and continue to evolve each day in our death.

Well, there aren't really days on this side, and time is hard to put into words, but for you guys, life is short. Special shout-out to my mom: I hope you find a good dude to settle down with soon because I only want you to be happy, mother!

And to all the other moms and dads reading this right now: remember to keep talking to us and writing to us and thinking about us! The more we hear from you, the better it is for all of us. We miss you as much as you miss us, and we're just gonna have to live with that for now. Well, at least you are.

Peace,
Robbie James Carlat

· 48 ·

Shadows and Light

Letting go of grief's pain while holding onto your child's heart was your first important choice. You've learned how to live with your loss and now it's time for what comes next. One thing is certain: wherever you look, you'll see shadows and light.

You've learned to embrace both at the same time. You've accepted your loss while maintaining your connection to your child. The bottomless pit of despair has been filled with bittersweet memories. Sorrow and joy have now become inseparable.

Shadows and light have also helped shape us. Devastation has made us resilient. The wreckage of our family has brought us closer together. Learning to be gentle with ourselves has allowed us to be more benevolent toward others. Facing what has scared us the most has made us fearless. Missing our child has left us with endless love.

Whenever I thought about Rob, it was a blend of shadows and light.

There was the happy light of our last Christmas together, accompanied by a shadow that he had made up his mind to kill himself.

There was the hopeful light of him at his first sober house, going to AA meetings and doing the steps, along with a shadow that he was merely complying because he had nowhere else to live.

There was the exquisite light of Rob being the sand and me being the water, coupled with a shadow that the sand often, and particularly at the end, made the water cry.

While Rob was alive, the dark shadows overpowered the occasional light. So a few months after he died, I tried to make myself feel better by giving Rob the halo he had never worn in life, but my sadness kept getting in the way. It felt like I was forcing myself to "snap out of it" and "get on with my life," as if I was racing against an imaginary heartache clock. Suffice it to say, I didn't know anything about grief back then.

A few years later, Rob's shadows and light had reached equanimity. I had made peace with their coexistence. Or so I believed. The truth was that Rob's many shadows—namely, all the shitty things he did and that happened to him in his life—began to bug me.

From the day we brought him home from Joplin, Missouri, until the day he died in Los Angeles, Rob was, as I wrote in his obituary, "a pain in the ass who was deeply loved by many." I realized I'd had enough of the "pain in the ass" part. I lived through it the first time around and had gone through it again and again after he died. I put in my ten thousand Rob "expert hours" and relived it to death.

Which led to another significant choice right before I started to write this book. I decided that I no longer needed to reexamine our past together. Death continues to reveal secrets, and I was so done with whatever revelations I might find. I let it go so I could stay in the light with Rob. I was fine with allowing the shadows to recede into the darkness.

Rob's beautiful spirit, which I met while tripping on magic mushrooms, is what I carry in my heart today. I chose to reframe the portrait of his life because it makes me feel good. It makes me feel good about Rob and about myself. I went a long time without feeling good and I'd like to go a long time in the opposite direction.

You may not need to do that with your child. I really hope you don't. I hope you had more light than shadows, and you've been able to fit both into your head and heart.

It really comes down to choosing your own perspective—and that got me thinking about art, which I know less than zero about. So I asked Janie, who recently took up drawing and is working on still lifes, to explain a bit about shadows and light.

"I find it helps to get some distance from the drawing," she said, delighted to be quoted in this book. "It makes it easier to see the depth and full dimension of the object and brings them to life."

That's exactly what I did with Rob, and I know his is a light that will never go out.

· *49* ·

It's Complicated

$\mathcal{W}$e all arrive at the Beginning at different times. There are many parents who for many reasons are still severely suffering the loss of their child after many years. Maybe they're stuck on a specific pain point, or maybe they've been in denial altogether, or maybe they suffer from depression or PTSD or any combination thereof. Any way you slice it, that's a lot of maybes to figure out.

Maybe you're one of those maybes, shaking your head and rolling your eyes right now because you're nowhere near any of this "letting go" and "moving forward" rigmarole I've been espousing. However long it's been since your child died, you're still hurting like it happened yesterday.

You don't know why you still feel this way or maybe you do and just refuse to acknowledge it. You feel helpless and hopeless, and the notion of accepting what has happened to your child feels as out of reach as the stars in the sky.

You're trapped in an insidious loop of guilt, anger, blame, and all the other usual trauma suspects, and as aggravating and heartbreaking as that is, it's still nowhere as intense and frightening as facing whatever it is that scares you the most.

You knew I was going to say that. You were waiting for it. And you also know that there's nothing I can say or do that's going to magically get you out of the endless cycle of mourning that prevents you from healing.

Your friends and family have undoubtedly suggested seeking professional help, and I'm with them 100 percent. I took Wellbutrin XL, which happens to be my size for most things, for about a year. It helped stabilize my mood and created something of a floor that prevented me from tumbling further into the grief abyss. My therapist Katarina turned out to be a godsend, instrumental in helping me navigate my heartache. Although I never felt especially stuck, I was a basket case when I first went to see her and was transformed for good by the time she sent me packing a year later.

Here's the thing: if you're hurting enough, you'll go for help, and if you're in denial enough, you won't. In the meantime, I have a few suggestions for those of you who are still struggling with what Katarina and her cohort like to call "complicated grief."

REVISIT YOUR STORY

I've done this countless times, traveling back to the day before Rob killed himself and also imagining the fateful night that followed. Every time I'm sitting with him at Din Tai Fung or picturing myself beside him on the couch right before he shot himself, the pain has gradually diminished. I know how brutal that sounds, but it was the only way I could reconcile with what Rob did. I was eventually able to let go of the anguish while holding my little boy asleep on the couch.

STAY CONNECTED

How you stay connected to your child is up to you. I write about Rob and talk to him every day. I feel his presence wherever I go. When I ask Zach about him, we generally share funny stories, and when I ask Caryn about him, we inevitably land on just how unfunny Rob could be. We are here and Rob is gone but we are still a family.

REMEMBER TO REMEMBER

I've chosen to focus on my happy memories of Rob. I've had enough of the unhappy ones to last several lifetimes. If you're going to be stuck, you might as well add things to the mix that make you smile. Rob is smiling in almost every old photo, and those memories last forever.

HAVE "THE TALK"

You may want to have a heart-to-heart with your child to metabolize your loss and see if you can find a measure of closure. I thought I'd check this out with Rob.

ME: Dude!

ROB: Yo!

ME: I have a few questions for you.

ROB: Shoot!

ME: Let's start with the most obvious: why?

ROB: Why what?

ME: You know what!

ROB: Pfft! You already know all the answers, dad! Haven't you been reading this book?

ME: I've been too busy writing it!

ROB: I know what you're trying to do! This is just an example to show your stuck readers how they can talk to their dead kids and get a little closure, right?

ME: Guilty as charged. What do you think they should ask their children?

ROB: I don't have a clue. What's gonna make them feel better?

ME: I don't know either. It's different for everybody.

ROB: Then what're you asking me for? They're gonna need to figure that out for themselves.

ME: That's my boy!

· 50 ·

Accidentally on Purpose

*W*hile Rob was alive, I never thought about being of service to others, mainly because I was always in service to him. As you've undoubtedly come to recognize by now, he was more than a handful, but once he was gone, I didn't know what to do with my hands.

Finding purpose, like so many facets of grief, is different for everyone. We all have to do our own soul searching and it took me a while to figure out mine.

I felt the whole "ticktock, life is short" thing and I didn't want to waste whatever time I had left on inconsequential nonsense . . . with the exceptions of playing Wordle and Connections every morning and listening to any number of sports and pop culture podcasts.

I thought about what Rob would want me to do and came up with a short list that he'd approve of:

1. Find happiness.
2. Enjoy the rest of your life.

I've accomplished number one and I'm still working on number two.

My initial soul searching led me to look at how I had changed post-Rob. I definitely felt more compassionate toward others and remember the exact moment when that happened. There was a homeless guy who slept outside in front of our garage in Venice and he'd ask me for spare change every morning, which I never gave him. After I came back from Rob's funeral in New York, I started giving him a few bucks every time he'd ask. He kept asking and I kept giving because . . . jeez, the dude slept outside every night! And there was a part of me that always worried that Rob would end up that way.

It's funny, I don't remember ever thinking "OMG! I have to find purpose and meaning in my life because otherwise what's the point of living?" Hadn't I already checked off most of Rob's list? It was hard to wrap my head around helping others because I was just too wrapped up in helping myself.

Little did I know I would find my purpose without looking for one, which has always been the way the universe has toyed with me. Everything changed one night near the end of our grief group, when I noticed a palpable lightness in the room. We still talked about the rough stuff, but the tone of our voices had shifted. We sounded calmer, more self-assured, and, dare I say it, hopeful. The vibe was just totally different from what it was in the early days when we were all such hot messes.

We had undergone a transformation, and although I was aware that it was occurring right under our noses, witnessing it that night sort of blew my mind. The proverbial light bulb went on, and that's when I knew I wanted to help other parents like us. It became a calling. I've never felt that way before, and it continues to surprise me to this day.

What I didn't know at the time was how much I would get out of it. Like I said, I was never a service-y type of guy. I'd occasionally donate to charity (primarily for tax purposes), but that was pretty much it. I was a bit of a selfish asshole back then and not especially evolved. I was completely clueless about helping others and its rewards, although it was vaguely familiar to me from learning about it in second grade.

I will simply say that sitting on the other side of the grief table and gently guiding other bereaved parents has been the most rewarding experience in my life. It is an honor and privilege to play a small part in their healing process, to say nothing of how it's helped my own well-being and growth as a slightly more evolved human.

Also, it feels really, really great!

There's a deep satisfaction in steering parents through the hell that we've all been through. Seeing the members of a grief group knit themselves together, care for each other, and ultimately transform is still astonishing, particularly since I've become a group leader, which means being fully present for someone, listening, empathizing, making room for his or her individual story—what we grief mavens call "holding space."

Working one-on-one as a grief coach has been rewarding in other ways. Sharing one's deepest and sometimes darkest thoughts with a kindred spirit who has had similar thoughts and feelings is as intimate as it gets. It often feels like open heart surgery, and I'm not always sure if I'm the doctor or the patient.

I look forward to listening to them. I look forward to asking them questions. I look forward to sharing whatever advice and wisdom I've learned along the way. I look forward to cracking jokes and laughing at theirs. I look forward to crying with them. I look forward to helping them to look forward themselves.

Moreover, I've become close friends with a few of the people I've helped over the years. I'm not their therapist, and they're not my clients. We're just fellow travelers who have met along the long and winding grief road, and I've learned as much from them as they have from me. I cherish these friendships; they're among a small handful of good things that have happened since my handful has been gone.

We're not only members of the same shitty club; we're family—and that means more to me than anything else in the world.

• 51 •

Do You Believe in Magic?

I didn't believe in much of anything before Rob died. I was never religious or spiritual, and the closest I ever got to God was to curse Him out when he finally granted seven-year-old Robbie's wish and took the sadness off of him twenty-one years later.

It was Rob's death that turned me into a believer. I went from thinking the light bulb goes out when we die (*that's all folks!*) to contemplating the existence of a phantasmagoric afterlife, not unlike Albert Brooks's take in *Defending Your Life*. I thought psychic mediums were basically grifters who preyed on people's grief but now know in my heart of hearts that Fleur is as real as real gets. I thought I'd never see Rob again—until I hung out with his spirit a few times while tripping. And I've also had some heated words with the Big Fella, whom I never believed in—but kinda/nearly/sometimes/maybe/almost do today.

I believe in these things simply because they provide great comfort and relief and just make me feel fine. I don't look too closely or question any of it anymore because . . . why should I? Believing in the supernatural, paranormal, mystical, and magical has opened me up to whole new worlds—wherever they may be. Knowing that Rob's spirit exists and is at peace on the other side of no tomorrow and that I'll see him again whenever I get there is nothing short of a miracle, which, of course, I also believe in.

There's no scientific proof of any of this ethereal stuff, especially for the dead interacting with the living, to which I respectfully retort, "Who cares?" I believe because I made the choice to. I chose to believe because not to believe hurt too much. I chose to believe just the way I chose to let go of the pain and suffering of losing Rob and also chose how to move forward with my life and turn my back on the past. I'm good with all of these decisions and strongly believe they were essential in my healing.

I'm not here to tell you what to believe in. That's your cross to bear. I'm merely suggesting that you keep an open mind and maybe look into a few of these otherworldly options. I understand if you're skeptical, because I was skeptical too, but why wouldn't you want to try something that can possibly give you peace of mind and help heal your heart?

After Rob died, I was walking around with a hole in mine and just wanted the pain of never seeing him again to stop. Despite joining a grief group and seeing a therapist, I felt hopeless and alone, and in those raw early months, I was open to any and all suggestions.

My search for otherworldly first aid began with Fleur, who promised to contact Rob's spirit, and she was as good as her word. She told me things that I thought she couldn't possibly have known, and she informed me that my father, who died shortly after my mom passed more than forty years ago, was there with Rob to help him transition to the other side. I burst into tears. My dad was a petty criminal who did time in prison while I was growing up. I had never cried for him before.

A few months later, a friend at the dog park confided that her brother had died by suicide, and she said that chanting had helped her. So I tried that, too. I wound up in her living room, chanting *Nam Myōhō Renge Kyō Nam Myōhō Renge Kyō*, which I still can't believe I agreed to. Near the end of the ceremony, there was a prayer for the deceased. I pictured Rob and began to chant louder, losing myself for just a few seconds, and then it was over, and I again bawled like a baby. Crying for Rob became the music of my broken heart.

It shouldn't have worked. All this was completely foreign to me. I'm a sixty-eight-year-old man from Brooklyn, a proudly cynical agnostic, and yet there I was: converted to LA woo-woo. It was this newfound faith that led me, a few years later, to tripping on psilocybin mushrooms, "dying," and communicating with the spirit of my dead son.

· 52 ·

How Psychedelics Helped
Heal My Broken Heart

$\mathscr{I}$ had done my share of recreational drugs, but psychedelics always seemed like a kaleidoscopic bridge too far. Between hearing about friends' bad trips and reading too much Hunter S. Thompson when I was young, I preferred to stay grounded on the lowest plane of consciousness. Maybe it boiled down to this: I was afraid of letting go.

After Rob died, there was nothing more to be afraid of and nothing of him to hold on to.

My way in through the doors of perception began with Netflix. Late one night I stumbled across *Fantastic Fungi*, an entertaining doc about my favorite pizza topping. It suggested that mushrooms and the mycelium network can heal and save the world, but I didn't really care about that. I was only interested in saving the little world of me.

When I told Janie, who had been gently nudging me toward exploring meditation and mindfulness, that I was seriously considering "tripping balls," she was psyched. She hooked me up with Lilah, a woman she knew from when she lived in Ojai, the premier woo-woo hotspot in Southern California.

In the months that followed, I went on three guided psilocybin journeys with Lilah, which is not her real name because magic mushrooms are still illegal in California. Trying to describe these journeys reminds me of what people said to me when Rob died—*there are no words*—and yet, here I go.

The first trip was a low-dose warm-up: two pieces of dark chocolate infused with 1½ grams of psilocybin mushrooms. This was just enough to produce a psychedelic experience replete with cascading colors, fractal patterns, trees pulsating with life, and a feeling of euphoria.

I loved every second of it. The third trip—4½ grams of raw psilocybin mushrooms dipped in honey—was a healing journey in which I saw what I can describe only as bird angel mechanics working on me with their tiny drills, fixing whatever they thought needed fixing. But it was the magical second trip—3 grams of mushrooms blended into a pineapple smoothie—that changed me forever.

On a beautiful weekday afternoon, I drove up the coast to Lilah's hideaway in Ojai. Lilah, a striking beauty in her early sixties, has been guiding spiritual seekers in the ways of "the medicine" for more than a decade. She's a warm, wise healer right out of central casting.

In her big backyard ("my garden of delight"), which is shaded by ancient oak and sycamore trees with giant branches that I've seen transform into octopus tentacles, we sat on the grass and discussed what's known as "set" and "setting." "Set" is simply stating your intentions—what you hope to get out of the experience—which, in my case, included the possibility of connecting with Rob. Anything beyond that would be, in nonpsychedelic terms, gravy. "Setting" refers to where you're doing this and who is guiding you.

After a half hour or so, we went back into the house, where I chugged the shroom smoothie and then lay down in "the temple," a big open room with pillows and blankets covering the floor. Lilah put on meditation music and told me to relax and wait for "liftoff," which she said could take up to an hour and can be physically intense.

Lying on my back looking at black marks on the pine ceiling, I became first sweaty and then cold and itchy. I'm not sure how much time passed, but eventually those marks began to swirl and then turned into hundreds of spiders skittering above me. The mushrooms had kicked in. Lilah suggested that I return to the garden and stretch out on the grass facing a Buddha statue under the giant oak. This is where shit got unreal.

Moments later, I died.

Let me explain. I was staring at the Buddha and then gazing up into the branches when everything started to move gradually toward me. I saw what looked like jigsaw puzzle pieces disengaging from each other, and then it felt like I was disintegrating and being taken away. Closing my eyes, I found myself in this buzzy white space, and after some time I opened my eyes and apparently shouted: "I just died and it was fuckin' beautiful!" I was absolutely giddy. Lilah, who had been sitting by my side the entire time, smiled. Then I told her that I was going back to the Buddha because I had noticed its face was slowly changing.

What I saw began as a blur, like a Polaroid snapshot, but when it came into focus, I knew right away that I was looking at Rob's spirit. He was wearing a beanie and John Lennon–style glasses and appeared as an old man with feline features, and I just started sobbing. I was looking at my boy's spirit, and it was the most beautiful thing I'd ever seen. Seconds later, his spirit started to grow and light up, and I said, "Oh my god, you have such a beautiful heart! I'm honored to be your dad. I love you, Robbie." I thanked him and told him how much I missed him every day.

Then the face of the Buddha went fuzzy again and another spirit appeared, one I recognized immediately. "Hi, Dad," I said. He was a handsome spirit, also with a big heart, and I told him that I could finally see what my mom saw in him. He looked sad, however. I told him it was okay, that I forgave him for everything. But when I tried to give him a hug, the Buddha's face changed back into Rob, slightly smirking, which was trademark Rob. My mom also dropped by to say hi, which made the comedown even more pleasant than usual.

The next day, after a mostly sleepless night, Lilah and I sat down in the garden for an "integration" convo, basically going over the previous night's highlight reel, reflecting on what I had learned, and discussing how I could take that back with me and integrate it into my daily life.

I had hit the magic mushroom jackpot. Seeing Rob's magnificent spirit gave me the peace and comfort I desperately needed. I'd also seen my parents: a reminder of where I came from. And then there was the quieting of my death anxiety when I seemingly "died." All told, I got more out of this journey than twenty-five years of talk therapy. It was the most profound and transformative spiritual experience in my life.

But I had a few questions for Lilah. Was any of what happened, you know, *real*? Was it magic? Was it the medicine? Was it just a home movie I made up in my altered state?

"The medicine always gives you what you need. You saw the truth. When we're in connection with our consciousness, it's all truth. It's all God. And it's all love," Lilah explained in a caring tone that inspired confidence.

She suggested that I focus on cultivating and nourishing these new insights and feelings in whatever ways would work best for me. "This

can be transformative if your integration is taken with some commit-
ment, but it's not unheard of to have this amazing experience and then
go back into your old patterns and habits," she cautioned. "That's why
people like to come back and do this again. They forget and the medicine helps them remember."

That's precisely why I was back at Lilah's house six months later,
this time joining five perfect strangers seeking whatever it was they were
looking for. I had forgotten a few things and needed a little help from
my psychedelic friends.

Back when I'd met with Fleur, the psychic medium, I'd asked her
what she saw in my future. "You will be a healer," Fleur said, "helping
other parents like yourself. And Rob will be working with their children
on the other side."

I sort of dismissed that at the time. Back then, I couldn't imagine
myself or Rob healing anyone. But about a year after my grief group
ended, I decided to become a grief counselor and coach. And yet, in
spite of this, I needed a spiritual tune-up.

Our little group of strangers sat crossed-legged on the floor while
Lilah introduced what we would be taking—a special formulation of a
plant called kanna, with a touch of MDMA added to give it that extra
kick. She explained that kanna has been used forever by the indigenous
people of southern Africa to induce euphoria, whereas MDMA allows
for "a softening around the heart, as well as clarity and insight."

We each took two pills and found a place to hunker down. "It
takes about an hour to feel the effects, so you may want to put one hand
on your heart and the other on your belly," said Lilah soothingly. Then
she recommended that we think about the people we love.

About forty-five minutes in, I was sweaty and tingly, two surefire
signs that the medicine was about to do its thing. Soon I started to smile,
and then I was grinning, and then I was beaming. I closed my eyes and
all I could see was Janie's smiling face, and I was filled with an immense
love for her.

That feeling grew stronger until I flashed on my younger son,
Zach, smiling hard as he often does, and I realized that these are the two
people I love most in this world. That led me straight to another world
where I saw Rob smiling back at me, and I was so happy to see him
again. Yes, I was feeling incredibly buzzed but also incredibly at peace.

He and I shot the shit, same as always, and then we just started laughing. It felt so good to be with him again. A photo of Rob and Zach from when they were teens flashed into my mind, and I started to think of other people I love and have loved. That was when my parents entered the picture. My father started to apologize for not being a good dad, but I assured him that I'd always love him for taking care of Rob when he crossed over, and I was overjoyed to see my mom, who thanked me for forgiving my dad.

Now I needed to ask Rob for a favor.

"Dude, can you do something for me? I've been talking with two fathers whose sons died recently and I wonder if you can check up on them and see how they're doing," I said a little too loudly, but no one in the room heard me because they were probably inside their own family portraits. I gave Rob the sons' names, and he said he'd be right back.

"They both said the same thing, Dad," Rob began. "They said they were sorry and not to worry because they're no longer in pain, and they love their dads, just like I love you. By the way, happy Father's Day!"

Rob appeared in the photo with his two new friends, and then their fathers came into focus with their arms around their sons. Other friends and family began to squeeze into what now looked like the *Sgt. Pepper* album cover but filled with people I love. I asked Rob if anyone was missing, and he just looked at me and smirked.

"Um, yeah, you fuckin' idiot!" he said, as only Rob could say it. "*You!*"

That's when a little boy wearing a winter parka and carrying a toy rifle walked into the photo—me when I was four years old—followed by an adorable little girl with pigtails who lives inside Janie's heart. She took the rifle, put it aside, and held hands with the little boy.

By now I was crying for joy. I felt so lucky to be loved and deeply in love, and it was in that moment that I knew my heart was finally healed. I was home.

• 53 •

Final Thirty-Second Time-Out

I'm taking my last thirty-second time-out to acknowledge that some of you may still be struggling with certain aspects of your grief and are having difficulty moving forward or are just taking more time to heal.

Don't be discouraged. Things will get better. There's no rush. Your grief is patient. It's not going anywhere. It'll be there whenever you're ready to engage with it. You're doing your best, even if it doesn't feel like it, and that's all you can do.

What I'd like to do is remind you of an important thing that you may have forgotten because it often gets lost in the grief sauce. I've repeated it throughout this book and I'm going to repeat it one more time for those of you who are still feeling blue and may need a little extra-special inspiration today. It's simply this: there is always hope.

I know it's hard to see sometimes. The sadness blinds us, but hope is always right there with you. All you have to do is reach out for it. Whenever you're having a really bad day, wrap your arms around it and don't let go. And it doesn't hurt to also hold on to it on the not-so-bad days as well.

Let hope guide you. Hope is the light in the darkness. Whatever you're feeling right now will pass. Things will get better, and then they'll get worse, and then they'll get better again . . . you know the drill. You've been on the exhausting grief ride for what feels like forever, but it's not forever. And as long as you have hope in your heart, everything is going to be okay because hope is everything.

We're getting to the end of this book, but that doesn't mean that you're getting to the end of your grief. As you well know by now, grief doesn't end. It just becomes a part of you. What does end is the pain—as long as you have hope.

And for those who need another bit of encouragement, here's one last thing.

I was walking on the beach the other day and saw a little boy in a wet suit coming out of the ocean carrying a small red pail filled with water. It took me a few seconds to notice he didn't have arms or legs (hands were attached to his shoulder and feet to his hips). What he did have was a look of sheer determination on his face, which just stopped me dead in my tracks.

I couldn't take my eyes off of him as he slowly made his way to the other kids waiting for him on the beach. When he got there, he dumped the water next to a sandcastle—just like I did all those years ago on the beach with Robbie—and then he turned right around and trudged back toward the ocean.

I was so moved by this kid, who couldn't have been more than five or six. He made me think about how people can endure almost anything. And then I thought of us, walking around every day with that same determined look in our eyes, and it just hit me that despite everything we've been through, life is beautiful.

Okay, time back in.

· 54 ·

Days of the Dead

$\mathscr{F}$rom time to time, you may feel the sting of your loss when you least expect it. You'll do your best to ride it out and then seamlessly return to whatever is going on in your life. Your love of your child never fades away, but at least twice a year, the loss feels like more than just a sting. It's a gut punch that brings you right back to the beginning of the end—the day your child died.

Unhappy death day! Unhappy birthday! What do you get a child who got everything you had to give?

Let's kick off the morbid festivities with the anniversary of your child's death. This day sucks, plain and simple. Leading up to this day sucks, and the days after this day suck. It doesn't matter if your child has been gone for one year or twenty-five, this is one of the worst days of the year, "celebrating" the worst day of your life.

Your family, friends, and some people you haven't heard from in a while will check in and ask how you're doing, and although they mean well, it just makes you feel worse because it reminds you of how terrible you felt the last time they asked you this incredibly obvious question.

You can try to distract yourself, but there's no avoiding it, and there's also no panacea for how you want to spend this melancholy day of the dead. Maybe you'll pay a visit to the cemetery or maybe you'll take a day off from work just to be alone with your thoughts. It really doesn't matter—you can't escape the dark cloud overhead. You'll do your best to weather the storm and hope that the sun'll come out tomorrow . . . and yech, how I hate that stupid song! The truth is that you'll get through it (I'm talking about the day, not the song) and carry on with your life until next year's "celebration."

189

On the one-year anniversary of Rob's death, I spent most of the day listening to Mac Miller's posthumous album *Circles* on a loop. Mac ODed a few months before Rob died, and Rob really loved Mac, so I've always associated the two of them with each other. The album is hauntingly sad and beautiful, and I've listened to it on every subsequent anniversary. When it comes to Rob, I'm a regular party animal!

And don't forget to wear your party hat for the fun and games of your child's actual birthday, the other worst day of the year, "celebrating" one of the best days of your life. Another year, another sucker punch in the face and a chance to revel in the tragic reality that your child will never grow old.

The buildup to these crappy days is often worse than the actual day itself, and I don't have any brilliant insights for how you should prepare for them. I can tell you that staying in bed for the day and hiding under the covers with Sweet Lady Jane triple berry birthday cake is not the worst way to go about it.

Rob was never a big fan of his birthdays, particularly when he was a little boy, howling his way through many of them. We always thought it was about adoption, and these celebrations just amplified his ineffable sense of abandonment. Now I know exactly how he felt.

For the last few years before his death, I'd call Rob on his birthday and goof on him for being an "old man." I can almost hear him laughing now. These days I call Zach and Caryn and we bum out for a bit and sometimes cry. It hasn't really gotten any easier and I suspect that it won't. It's just a brutal reminder of how much we love and miss him, and how much we'd rather have him here with us. No one liked to party as much as Rob, but even he would find his birthday to be a drag.

I then look at photos of birthdays past, and Rob's smiling and mugging for the camera in almost every one of them. Boy, do I miss that smile! He chilled out about these celebrations as he grew older. During his teenage years, we generally marked the occasion by doing the standard birthday commemoration—eating pizza, singing the stupid song, and blowing out the candles on a giant chocolate chip cookie cake that Caryn had baked and that we all loved. Then it would be time for the funny cards, with funnier things we wrote inside of them, and we'd top it off by giving him increasingly lavish gifts, which culminated in a tricked-out Ford Focus when he turned seventeen. These were mostly happy days.

When he lived in LA, Maura and I celebrated one of his birthdays by taking him out to an old-school red-sauce Italian restaurant in our neighborhood that served unlimited garlic knots. We didn't get together with him for his next birthday, when he turned twenty-eight, because he was busy either working or going to a meeting; I've forgotten what his excuse was. Of course, I had no idea that that would be the last one.

One of the happiest days of my life is now one of the saddest. There are no balloons, no funny cards, no cake, and no Rob. At the end of the day, I blow out the imaginary candles for him and make a wish, knowing that it can't possibly come true.

A Life in a Flash

*R*ight before you die, your life supposedly flashes before your eyes like an extended version of a bar mitzvah montage, with Green Day's "Time of Your Life" playing in the background.

I've often wondered what that flash would look like. Does it start with the day you were born and move forward chronologically? Or does it do a Benjamin Button and go in reverse? Does it follow a narrative arc, or is it just random moments in time? And how does our mind shoehorn an entire life in a flash when it takes more than three hours to watch any Oscar-worthy biopic?

One thing I know for sure is that we've all seen countless cuts of our child's movie. It's usually a midnight show or thereabouts, and despite knowing there's no possibility of a happy ending, we can't take our eyes off the screen. We can recite every line of dialogue and we know every set and location of every scene, and even though it breaks our heart, we can't stop watching it over and over again.

Frankly, I've had enough of these late-show tearjerkers, and maybe you have too. Now playing nightly in the Larry Theater of my mind is a more Hallmark-y, feel-good version of the flash that was our life together, and you'll always find me sitting in our favorite seats in the center of the top row.

Robbie is nine days old and he's lying by my side as we watch Bills place-kicker Scott Norwood prepare to break my heart and win Super Bowl XXV against my beloved Giants with a last-second field goal attempt.

I tell Robbie that we're going to win this game because he's my lucky charm, and when the kick sails wide right and the Giants miraculously win their second Super Bowl 20–19, I pick up my new baby boy, kissing and hugging him while we dance around our living room, celebrating a lot more than just winning the championship.

Rob is twenty-seven and Zach and I are taking him to see his first pro basketball game in person, the Clippers against the Nuggets, and when we get to Staples Center, it turns out that two of our three seats are together and the other one is across the aisle, so the kids sit next to each other and I'm the odd man out. I wind up watching them more than the game, which turns out to be a Clippers blowout after Jokić gets tossed, and they're cracking up and goofing on each other while I'm beaming because I can feel how much they love each other.

Robbie is eight and we're walking in the parking lot of Jones Beach Theater on our way to see my favorite band, Steely Dan, and he's with me because Caryn didn't want to go and he didn't want me to go alone. I have my arm around his shoulder and I'm overwhelmingly happy that he's with me. It's one of those perfect summer nights with a warm breeze coming off the ocean, and right before we get to security, some half-drunk, wholly stoned woman wearing a *Two Against Nature* T-shirt turns around and kneels down to talk with Robbie. She asks him what his favorite Steely Dan song is, and Robbie, without hesitation, says, "Rose Darling," which is kind of an obscure deep cut, and the woman bursts out laughing and says, "Your daddy taught you right, little boy!"

Rob is twenty-six and he's in our house in Venice to meet his new little bro, Wallace, an adorably devilish Jack Russell puppy. Wallace is frantically jumping all over him on the couch, so Rob scoops him up in one hand and places him on his belly and says, "Who's a good boy, Wallace, who's a good little boy?" Then Rob picks him up and brings him face-to-face and they kiss and lick each other, and I'm in the kitchen watching the two of them, quietly repeating to myself, "Who's a good little boy?"

Robbie is seven and sitting on my lap in his Teenage Mutant Ninja Turtles pajamas playing an interactive computer game called *Full Throttle*, and he's all excited as we help Ben, the leader of a biker gang, kick all kinds of ass at each gnarly obstacle thrown his way until we can't figure out how to climb over a warehouse fence guarded by an angry attack dog, so we switch to *Dust* and immediately encounter gunslingers, gold prospectors, and numerous hot babes in a Western saloon. Just as we're ready to face off in a duel with the Kid, a hot babe in my bedroom upstairs yells at us to go to sleep already, and we quietly laugh and stay up way past our bedtimes, playing these games late into the night.

Rob is twenty-seven, and we're riding a rickety elevator that leads to his new apartment on the sixth floor of a historic landmark building right on the waterfront in downtown Long Beach. I've never seen him look any prouder, and as soon as we walk in, I tell him that this is his dream place and that it reminds me of my first apartment and that I'm so proud of him. He's nodding and smiling hard, and the whole thing feels like we're in some type of an alternate Rob universe, and I've never felt more hopeful for him and think that maybe things will work out this time, and I get all caught up in his California dream.

· 56 ·

The Return of Joy

You've heard me say that you need to move through grief to get to the other side, but I haven't fully explained what happens once you make it through. That's when you discover that your grief has moved in and taken up permanent residence. It can't replace the space in your heart that died along with your child, but it can make you feel whole again.

So how, exactly, did you and your grief end up becoming such bosom buddies? Well, your first clue is that you're different. Your grief has made you at once stronger and softer. You're laughing and crying more easily, and the things that made you cry before don't hurt as much or for as long as they used to (which is not to say those things no longer hurt). You also see the world differently than you previously saw it. You sincerely care about the people in your life and the things that really matter, and you no longer have time for the things that don't.

Your second clue is that you're able to endure your sadness in a whole new way. Whenever you talk about your child, it's not as gut wrenching or debilitating as it was before because you've endured the worst pain that's ever been dished out. You're no longer feeling all of the shitty feelings from the early days because you've processed, adjusted, accepted, integrated—whatever word salad you want to call it, you've done it. You've done the work, you've moved through it, and you've listened to your heart.

The third clue is that you're back to living in the world the way you were living in it before your child passed away. You're going out to dinner with friends again, you're working out at the gym, swimming, doing yoga, or whatever you used to do to stay in shape. You're fully reengaged at work, or you're busy traveling, or you're reaping the rewards of volunteering. You're meditating or reading or praying or, if you're like me, just feeling the cool sand beneath your feet at the beach. Once again, we're absorbed in everything life has to offer and our grief is now along for the ride.

But the single biggest clue, the one that comes as such a pleasant surprise, is the return of joy. The first time it hits you, the first time you feel it deep in your heart again, you'll want to cry, and that may also be the first time in a long time that you're crying happy tears.

Just the thought of happy tears after all the unhappy ones I've shed was a great big hint that my grief and I would be eternally joined at the hip. It happened on the day of the unveiling of Rob's headstone, a little more than a year after he died. Going to the cemetery kinda sucked, but it was nice to see the sunflowers, four-leaf clover, and his favorite tattoo, "Life Rolls On," engraved on his memorial. We went with Rob's friends to this dive bar in Huntington right afterward, and did what Rob would've wanted us to do—we got shit-faced.

I'm usually a cheap date, but we all did tequila shots and toasted Rob with each one while his friends told funnier and more outrageous stories about him as the night wore on (none of which can be repeated here). It was just a great celebration of Rob's life, and it felt like he was right there with us.

I was laughing and crying all night long, and the room was just overflowing with love and joy. I remember feeling like George Bailey at the end of *It's a Wonderful Life*, so happy to be alive and so happy to be there with these people I adore, and from that happy moment on, I knew that everything was going to be okay.

It took another year for me to fully get there and it may take you longer, but you will get there and once you do, there's no turning back.

Becoming Extraordinary

*W*hen your child dies, you're no longer an ordinary parent. You become *extra* ordinary. The extra is the sorrow and suffering you must face and move through. Once you come out from the other side of this misery, you are permanently changed. You've gone from *extra* ordinary to extraordinary. Closing up the space between those two words has inexplicably opened up your brave new heart.

A piece of you is missing, but in its place is something different that has its own singular beauty. You now have the noble heart of a warrior. You are fearless, forthright, well grounded, and at peace. Your heart is healed and your empathy knows no bounds. You can speak only the truth because you know everything else is just noise. You are wiser and have learned things about life and death that most people could never imagine.

You can't see this transformation while it occurs, just like a caterpillar can't see that it's becoming a butterfly. You weren't even aware that it was going on, which is the only way it could've happened, and at the same time you alone made it happen.

It seems like everything about you is different, yet you are who you've always been—just more enlightened. You're the 3.0 version of yourself (my friend Tony likes to call me Larry3000), an advanced and enhanced parent with an unmatched ability to connect, especially to others just like you. That connection is extraordinarily solid, sincere, considerate, and heartfelt—a perfect reflection of who you have become.

The thing about being extraordinary is that you don't walk around feeling extraordinary. You wake up in the morning, get out of bed, go to work, come home, eat dinner, watch TV, go to sleep, and basically live your life the way you've always lived it. Your secret identity remains concealed. Sometimes you share it with others, but you mostly keep it to yourself. You're okay with being Clark Kent because you know Superman lives inside you.

Your child knows this, too. One of your unique superpowers has been the ability to reestablish a whole new relationship with them. You're now in touch with their authentic self because your hearts are doing the talking. You talk about whatever it was you always talked about, you ask advice, you gossip, or you just shoot the shit. You tell them how much you love and miss them, and they tell you the same, and you do this every day until you meet again, and for that reason alone, you love this superpower best of all.

One of the unanticipated benefits of being an extraordinary parent is that you're now an exclusive member of a private club. Whenever you meet another EP, you instantly recognize each other and talk in a kind of shorthand that only the two of you can understand. You are kindred spirits who are connected to each other, and your children's spirits are united on the other side. The wonderful and surprising reward of being in this club is how good it feels to listen to and help a fellow member.

Perhaps the most valuable benefit is what you've learned. You've learned that life is short and precious. You've learned that if you love, you grieve, and that love never dies. You've learned to listen to your heart even after it was obliterated. You've learned that you can be happy again despite missing your child more than anything. You've learned that your child's death was just the beginning of the next chapter of your life.

The funny thing about being extraordinary is that everybody you know already knows that you are. They've seen it every day since the day your child died. You were the last to know.

· 58 ·

The Final Lesson

*W*hen I was a kid in sleepaway camp, we had something called "general swim." We all had to pick a "buddy," and when the swim counselor blew his whistle, you had to grab your buddy's hand and raise your arms together, assuring the owners of the camp that you haven't drowned.

Wouldn't it be great if there was something like this for grieving parents who feel like they're drowning? Well, there is, and it starts with you!

Once you've been through what you've been through, you're as much of an "expert" on how to cope with your grief as I am. You've learned so much and now it's time for the final lesson—paying it forward and helping other bereaved parents navigate the long road ahead of them. Who knows this rocky terrain better than you?

I can't tell you how many parents like us I've spoken to over the years. My friends all know that I'm open to chat with anyone who's suffered the same fate as we have, and they've told their friends and so on and so on. It's an ever-widening circle, and you need to be a part of it.

You're not providing therapy, and it's nothing like being in a grief group. You're just a shoulder to lean on, a friend who will listen, understand, and, when appropriate, share some hard-earned wisdom. You're reassuring others that whatever they're feeling is "normal" and that they're not alone. You become a guide—a grief buddy—telling them what they can expect when they expect to cry forever.

Remember how you felt right after your child died? Your family and friends were there for you, but after a while, you felt like you were inflicting your pain on them, to say nothing of how impossible it was

201

for them to understand what you were feeling. It's just not the same as talking to someone who has walked in your shoes.

After Rob died, the only person I could talk to was Caryn. She was the only other person in the world who was feeling exactly what I was feeling. And even though we had each other, we both sometimes needed more. Boy, do I wish I had known the guy writing this book back then!

The relationship is similar to being an AA sponsor, except that it's totally okay if you want to chat over drinks. What makes it similar is that it's mutually beneficial. There's healing on both sides of this pairing, and the stronger the bond, the stronger the sense of intimacy, the stronger the exchange of knowledge, the stronger you both become.

But to be honest, there's more upside for you. Helping another parent like us is one of the most gratifying feelings you'll ever feel. It gives you a new sense of intention and meaning that you never could have imagined before. At least I couldn't.

I've been talking to my friend Steve, who lives in New York, for the better part of three years. We speak about our lost sons, our other children, and how we want to live the rest of our lives. Every time we hang up, I'm filled with a mix of satisfaction and affection for him that brings me to tears (the happy ones). He's become a close pal and I look forward to every one of our calls.

A few months ago, he told me that he had spoken to a colleague whose son recently died of fentanyl poisoning, and how afterward he had the giddy sensation that I just described.

"I've never felt so qualified to help people, no less in the darkest times they will ever know," Steve explained. "I emerged with enough perspective and humility to know that while I can't make it all better, I sure as hell can provide a comfortable shoulder and connection."

I've had similar conversations with people I've helped who went on to help others, and they've all reported the same thing. And that's the way the circle expands.

Not only are you paying it forward, but helping others also helps your own grief evolve. Guiding other bereaved parents on their maiden journey allows you to see your own trek from another perspective. It offers the distance you need to see what you went through in a more dispassionate light and often provides new clarity and insight. As strange as this may sound, it's a win-win at the highest level of loss.

There's one last thing I like to think about, and I'd like you to think about it too. Whenever I'm talking to other parents like us, I always think that Rob is in touch with their kids on the other side. I picture them hanging out, talking about us, laughing together, and then I hear the words, the words that I so desperately need to hear—*I love you, Dad*—and then everything feels all right.

· 59 ·

Me and Him

A Conversation with God

I've always had a hard time believing in God, particularly after Rob died. Even when I was cursing Him out, it just felt like I was talking to myself. So instead of checking in with you for our last goodbye, I thought it was finally time for me and Him to have a little sit-down and settle our differences, man to creator of the universe.

ME: Hello? Hi? Anybody home?

HIM: *Who goes there?*

ME: It's Larry. Shouldn't you have known that?

HIM: *Come back tomorrow!*

ME: But I'm here now.

HIM: *Do not arouse the wrath of the great and powerful Oz! I said come back tomorrow!*

ME: What are you talking about?

HIM: Ha! I'm just playing with you, Lar. Relax. Take a load off. What can I do you for?

ME: Well, first of all, I'm not sure if I even believe in you. And second of all, if you do exist, let's just say that I've never been one of your biggest fans.

HIM: I totally—and when I say totally, I mean encompassing all knowledge of the universe past, present, and future—understand. What's on your mind, my son?

ME: That's what's been on my mind—my son! And I've hated you ever since you took him from us!

HIM: I get it, Lar. You loved Rob like nothing else. You were a great father and did everything you could've done for him.

ME: And then you took him away!

HIM: I can see why you feel that way, again, because of the whole omniscient thing, but you already know why Rob is no longer with you. You said it yourself.

ME: I wish I knew what you were talking about.

HIM: It's in part II of this book. By the way, I love what you're doing here. Although I was less than thrilled with that angry "vengeful motherfucker" crack. That one was *no bueno, mi amigo.* Otherwise, very powerful stuff. Will help a lot of people. You wrote, and I quote, "The soul knows when it's time to go." And that's it. That's all there is to it. *The great and powerful Oz has spoken!* Love that movie! I've seen it like a billion times!

ME: But why didn't you let me help Rob?

HIM: He didn't want me to. He had made up his mind. He no longer wanted to be. It was just too difficult and painful for him.

ME: What about all the other children you've taken away too soon?

HIM: There have always been a lot of people who are angry with me. They blame me for all kinds of stuff, but the truth is that none of it is my doing. Well, that's not entirely true. I created all life on Earth, but then things began to, as the saying goes, take on a life of their own. I'm not the grand puppet master everybody makes me out to be. You people have free will.

ME: But what about the pain and suffering you've caused everyone reading this book? You've broken our hearts and made us all miserable beyond belief.

HIM: Hmm . . . beyond belief. Interesting choice of phrase there, my son. All I can tell you is that's just the way life works. It's just a big bowl of randomness. I know that's not what you want to hear, but shit happens. Things change.

ME: Goddamn it!

HIM: Jesus H. Christ! Haven't you ever heard of the third commandment? Lemme make it easier for you. Just call me OMG.

ME: Now I know you don't exist! You sound just like me!

HIM: But secretly, when all is said and done, you'd like to believe that I do exist. You need to believe in Me because it makes you feel a tiny bit better about Rob. If you believe in Me, you can also believe that Rob is in a better place and that he's no longer hurting, and that's consoling and better than believing in nothing.

ME: I already know that Rob is at peace, and you had nothing to do with it!

HIM: Dude, who do you think made those magic mushrooms?

ME: Touché. So as long as I'm in your divine presence, what can you tell people about grief that they don't already know?

HIM: Well, I don't like to brag, but I am all knowing. That's why they never let me on *Jeopardy!*

ME: Okay, so impart some of that famous wisdom and knowledge that we've heard so much about.

HIM: Well, you've already done that for me! You're my instrument! You've been nurturing others! You've been sharing your experiences! You've been helping those in need, my son!

ME: Stop calling me that! I'm not your son!

HIM: "I am He as you are He as you are me and we are all together." Love those lads! They still hold up, still my best work. Along with the Serenity Prayer and pizza.

ME: You're a pretty funny guy for being God.

HIM: Wanna hear a joke?

ME: Shoot.

HIM: What's the difference between Me and Bono?

ME: Tell me.

HIM: Rob has never met Bono.

ME: Ha! That's pretty good! I guess I can see how you'd get along with Rob.

HIM: Are you kidding? I love that kid! He makes me laugh like no one else and has such a big heart.

ME: Okay, Mr. Mysterious Ways . . . are you me? Or are you just one of the voices in my head?

HIM: What's the difference? How does this convo make you feel?

ME: It makes me feel okay, I guess.

HIM: Why?

ME: Maybe because it gives me hope. Maybe believing in You makes me feel less afraid of death. Maybe it takes away some of the horribleness of losing Rob. Maybe believing in You provides a little comfort.

HIM: Maybe believing in yourself does too.

ME: Amen, brother. Last question: will I ever see Rob again?

HIM: I could tell you, but then I'd have to kill you. Hahahaha! Peace out, dude! See ya soon!

· 60 ·

Life Rolls On

$\mathcal{W}$elcome! Welcome! Welcome! You made it! I'm so glad to see you here! I wish I could give you a great big hug! Pour yourself a drink, put your feet up, and enjoy the moment. No one deserves it more than you!

You've been through a lot and have come a long way. As time goes by, the early days of your grief have become fuzzy. You remember the pain, but you don't *really* remember. It's sort of like how some women forget the intensity of childbirth (or so I've been told). They forget the physical pain but not the memory of it.

That's why it's important to take a look at how you and your grief have changed. It's truly amazing, almost magical when you look back on it. You've progressed from feeling completely hopeless and in the worst pain you've ever felt in your life to cherishing each day you have left.

How the hell did that happen?

You know how, but even that begins to fade. All the hard work you've put in, all the tears you've shed, all the dark nights of the soul you've wrestled with get packed away in your head and heart because the worst is over, and life rolls on.

Whenever I think of those three little words, I think of Rob. I see those words tattooed in cursive on his left forearm. When he was here with us, I thought those words were emblematic of his no-fucks-given attitude, but now I think they're a message to me and a message to you.

The message is something we all know and have always known, and I don't think I need to spell it out for you, because I think we all feel it deep down inside. We live our lives differently than we have in the past and differently than others who have never experienced anything like the depth of our loss.

209

For us, Life Rolls On has become a way of life. We need to do things that feel important to us and to others. We are more present, slowing life's roll and amplifying each moment. We appreciate every day we have left on Earth and the day ahead, whenever it comes, when we meet our child again.

We still curse out idiot drivers who cut us off on the freeway, we talk too loud and too much on our phones like everybody else, and we often forget to replace the toilet paper roll. We're not perfect. We fuck up like everyone else. We're extraordinary but we're also human.

Which, again, is absolutely remarkable given the trauma and drama we've endured. We're still standing and doing our best, and that's what our kids would want us to do. I know this and you know this because that's what they tell us every day.

They remind us to be happy, they remind us to be kind, they remind us to be grateful, they remind us to be honest, they remind us how much love we have in our hearts and how we should spread it around far and wide but also leave a little leftover for ourselves.

And that's what I'm going to remind you about right now.

Do me a favor and close your eyes. Picture your child's smiling face. Stay with it a moment. Breathe it in. Savor it. Have you ever seen a more beautiful face? Now I want you to remember the day they were born and the first time you set eyes on them and how it was love at first sight. Remember their gorgeous tiny face, and remember how incredible you felt on that wonderful day. Breathe that day in as much as you can.

Now fast forward to another happy time in their life. Maybe it was a birthday or a trip to Disneyland or a day at the beach. Picture how happy they look blowing out the candles or frolicking in the waves or whatever they're doing in the joyful moment you've chosen. Now place your hand over your heart and feel them smiling and saying, "Hi Mom! Hi Dad!" Have you ever seen a happier face?

Okay, now take a deep breath and imagine their face today. They look all grown up, with a beatific grown-up smile, but if you look closely, you can still see the baby that lives inside them. Now tell them how much you miss them. Say the words out loud. And tell them how much you love them and will always love them. Say it over and over again until you can hear them saying it back to you. Smother them with kisses and hug them tight. Feel their heart beating next to yours. Feel their tears running down your cheek. Now, as gently as you can, let them go and whisper, "Goodbye."

Open your eyes.

Epilogue

Almost twenty-five years after I wrote my first letter to Rob for *Esquire*, I wrote a second. I think it's a good place to end.

Dear Rob,

I love you, Dad.

Those are the last words you said to me the day before you killed yourself.

They're also the last words you said to me in the first letter I wrote to you, twenty-five years ago. Back then you were "Robbie," and I was "Daddy," and I never thought I could possibly love you more than I did. Then again, I never imagined I'd be writing this letter to you now.

At least, not consciously. But deep down, I came to fear this day would come. On some level, I felt that, no matter how hard I tried, there was nothing I could do to stop it.

The letter I wrote when you were seven was about how I hadn't wanted to adopt you—it was Mom's idea—and how that feeling vanished the moment I first saw your beautiful face.

This letter is about another kind of feeling, one that will never vanish.

Sometimes I feel that you're right here beside me. I hear you talking to me—like right now I just heard you say, "Dad, I hate it when you sound so sad. That's the worst."

It's the worst for me too, dude. There was a whole lot of "the worst" those last few years. Ending with the worst of the worst. Which I didn't see coming when we had lunch at our favorite Chinese restaurant in Los Angeles the afternoon before you did what you did.

We ate soup dumplings and talked about the usual random bullshit—how we were both rooting for Tyrion and Arya to be the last two standing on *Game of Thrones* and how we both loved new songs by Watsky, Boogie, 2Young, and other names I'd never heard of before your brother Zach, ever the family DJ, turned us on to them—and though you looked exhausted from juggling three minimum-wage kitchen gigs, it felt like just another day.

I knew you were having a rough time and owed a bunch of money to the kind of person no one should owe money to, but you uncharacteristically insisted that you didn't want my help. That should've been my first clue. Then you mentioned something about going backpacking in Europe with your cat, Biscuit, or maybe joining the navy.

I don't remember what else we talked about, but I do recall how nice you were to our waitress, who was wearing a "trainee" tag. You were always kind and courteous to servers in restaurants and insisted that I tip at least 20 percent. "Cough up a buck, you cheap bastard," you deadpanned, quoting from *Reservoir Dogs*, a Carlat family film festival staple.

It wasn't until you said my four favorite words and walked away from my car that I realized something was different. You seemed to be moving in slow motion. I remember noticing your dirty desert boots with the broken laces. You looked small and defeated. It was like with each step, you were becoming my little boy again.

I wish God would take the sadness off of me.

You said those words when you were seven, and He made you wait twenty-one years to get your wish. I've always believed we come into this world fully baked, and you came in howling. You were a cranky baby, a difficult child, an angry teenager, a volatile adult, and an unreliable narrator every step of the way. You were depressed for as long as I can remember and struggled with drugs, alcohol, and bipolar disorder from your late teens until you shot yourself. You were such a pain in the ass. . . .

. . . And yet I adored you. Because you were also sweet, charming, sensitive, whip-smart, and funny as hell. When you laughed, it felt like all was right with the world. And nothing pleased me more than one of your wisecracks that sounded just like me.

I love Zach and Mom with all my heart, but there was something especially intense about my love for you. Maybe it's because you needed it so much. No one in the world is easier and more loveable than Zach. I rarely worried about him, but I was forever trying to rescue you.

Yet I didn't want you to follow me to LA, where Maura and I were starting a new life after Mom and I divorced. I warned you it was expensive, that it would be tough to find a job and impossible to get around without a car. I told you that you couldn't live with us in Venice because Maura worked from home and we didn't have a spare room.

What I didn't tell you was the truth. I was almost as big a liar as you were, but we lied for different reasons. Mine were lies of omission. I was scared that if I told you what I really thought about what you were doing or not doing, you'd cut me out of your life. I was scared that I'd lose you and that you'd be lost and alone.

Still, our lies had a certain symmetry: I lied to protect you, and you lied to protect me.

When you eventually did come to live with Maura and me, it kinda sucked and was kinda nice. It kinda sucked because you disrupted our life and amped up my anxiety to eleven. And it was kinda nice simply because we got to spend so much time together.

The nice part seems even nicer now. As for the suck part, I had no idea what "suck" really meant back then.

It was especially nice watching you cook. I loved when Maura called you "the kitchen elf." Do you remember the night you prepared that special meal for us? We went to Whole Foods and bought a Flintstones-sized chunk of rib eye and a bunch of veggies (mainly for Maura) and then picked up a bottle of bourbon. That made me uncomfortable, but you assured me that the whiskey would burn off and give the dish a rich, sweet flavor.

While you were prepping, I looked in occasionally to make sure you weren't sneaking any of the alcohol. Finally, you brought out your pièce de résistance, and it was absolutely . . . disgusting! The meat was so drenched in bourbon that we could barely choke it down. Of course, we told you it was delicious, the way I used to rave about anything you accomplished when you were a little boy.

Goddamn it, Rob! Not a day goes by that I don't miss the hell out of you. I miss us hanging out and singing the Thundercat song ("I wish I had nine lives . . .") and the way we'd sing the "meow" part together. I miss shooting pool with you in that shitty bowling alley in Torrance, and I miss secretly loving it when you beat me. I miss hearing you say "Yo" and us bumping fists. I miss you whipping out one of your Bad Motherfucker wallets, which you constantly lost, proving that you were anything but. I miss walking around the Del Amo mall, with my arm around your shoulders the day before you killed yourself, thinking that things would somehow get better, which of course they didn't.

When I think about our lives together, you know what makes me sad? I just heard you answer: "Everything?" And that's not far from the truth. But more than anything, I wish we had more joy.

A while ago, at the end of a meeting of my grief group, a moderator asked everybody to share happy memories of our kids when they were little. One by one, the grieving parents recalled Hawaii vacations, birthday celebrations, Little League games, normal family stuff. But when it was my turn,

I drew a blank. It was a daily shit show at our house right up until you fell asleep at night. And then I told them about Disney World.

All I remember was you crying nonstop. While Mom and Zach went on the rides, we watched from the ground, me desperately trying to distract you from whatever demon was upsetting you. Aside from one shot of you eating a churro, the photos from that Florida trip have a consistent theme: Zach beaming in Magic Kingdom heaven and you looking miserable in Mickey Mouse hell.

Years later I asked what you remembered about Disney World. You said it was the best time we ever had as a family.

The irony of that cracks me up, but so many other things break my heart—like the fact that I have so little that belonged to you. I left the bulk of your stuff in your Long Beach apartment, including that oddball collection of about two hundred BIC disposable lighters. All I took was twenty of your crazy-ass T-shirts, which I sent to Mom, who had them sewn into a memorial quilt.

Quick funny story: when I came down to the lobby with those T-shirts in a plastic trash bag, I ran into Theresa, the building manager. "I'm so sorry for your loss, Mr. Carlat," she said. "Rob was such a good guy."

"Thank you," I said.

"You know, a lot of people wanted that apartment, but we let Rob have it because he was so nice and smart and charming," she continued, "and because he was a cancer survivor."

Dude, I nearly burst out laughing when I heard that lie.

In addition to the T-shirt quilt, I have one saved voicemail from a few years back. It lasts all of ten seconds and it's just you saying, "Hey, happy birthday. Gimme a call back. Love you. Bye." Full disclosure: I sometimes listen to that voicemail when it's not my birthday.

I also carry a Robbie memento on my keychain: a six-month sobriety chip from the only AA meeting you invited me to. It was the one time you really gave the program a shot, and I remember the leader asking if there was anyone celebrating six months sober. You stood up and smiled, and I could see that you were trying to contain it, to look cool, but pride beamed out of you like sunlight breaking through clouds.

Of course, I started crying, just as I'm crying now. You accepted the chip while everyone applauded. Then you returned to your seat, handed me the chip—the greatest gift imaginable—and said, "Happy Father's Day."

You always hated it when I told you how much I worried about you, but I had no choice. I worried when you wailed endlessly as a baby. I worried when you didn't have many friends in grade school. I worried when you flipped out at seventeen and had to be hospitalized. I worried when you left

Long Island for the first time to move upstate. And I worried when you told me that you were moving to LA and every day after that, until we ran out of days.

"You can stop worrying now, Dad," I just heard you whisper, and I won't argue with that. But here's another truth: I'd give anything to have one more day of worrying about you.

I often wonder what you were thinking on that terrible night. According to police and coroner's reports, you were hammered on Hurricane malt liquor (it surprised me that no drugs were found) and playing video games with two friends from AA. They ducked out for a minute, and that's when you ducked out forever. I don't think you were thinking about anything more than making the pain stop. I've pictured you playing with the gun (that was another surprise), putting it in your mouth, closing your eyes, and silently saying, "Peace out."

As if that image isn't upsetting enough, this appeared in the police report: "Upon officers' arrival on scene, the decedent's cat was on top of the decedent licking his hands."

When I read that, I knew that you did what you did "accidentally on purpose." There was no way that you'd *plan* to leave Biscuit behind. You had rescued her, but she couldn't rescue you. In that moment, you weren't thinking about your cat or how killing yourself would break the hearts of everyone who loved you. It was an opportunistic and impulsive act. Still, if it didn't happen that night, it no doubt would've happened down the line. With all the close calls you had in the past, it was amazing that it hadn't happened already.

That reminds me of the first close call. Not long after we bought your first car, you got into a major accident, the first of many. Mom and I jumped into my SUV and raced to the scene. It was pouring rain, and I remember seeing the flashing lights of a fire truck and an ambulance and thinking that this wasn't going to end well. Then we saw your Ford Focus, T-boned and crushed like an accordion, but there was no sign of you or your girlfriend, whose name I've forgotten. Mom and I were freaking out, and I bolted out of the car and ran to the ambulance, where I saw your girlfriend lying on a stretcher wearing a neck brace. You were next to her, with some bruises on your forehead, but not really looking much worse for wear. When I asked if you were okay, you replied, "I'm invincible!" I never wanted to slap some sense into you more than at that moment.

You scared the shit out of me, Rob. You were fearless, reckless, and self-destructive—a recipe for disaster that often took you right to the edge. Like the time you made a daredevil leap from the second floor of a parking garage—Wile E. Coyote running off a cliff—and broke your left leg, pelvis, and I don't remember how many other bones. (I'll never forget how you cursed out the doctor when he tried to remove the staples from your leg and how you wound up taking them out yourself.) Man, it sucks being scared of someone you love. And it sucks even more when that someone is your little boy.

You are the sand, little boy, and I will always be the water.

That's a line from the first letter I wrote to you. It refers to a day at your Uncle Stephen's beach where I tirelessly poured water into what was supposed to be a moat surrounding a sandcastle. The sand immediately drank up the water, but I kept at it, refilling the bucket and pouring in more water, determined to keep you happy and make everything perfect. I had that line tattooed on my left forearm a few months after you permanently left us. In fact, we all got tattoos in your memory—Mom and Zach as well as me—like we needed another reminder of how you got under our skin.

There's something I never told you—or anyone else, for that matter. It was the second time you threatened to kill yourself (a year before you made good on that threat), when you came to my house in the middle of the night to say goodbye forever, and I wouldn't let you inside because I was doing the whole "detaching with love" thing. We shook hands, as if we'd come to a formal agreement, and you walked away, becoming smaller with each step. That's when I had the horrible thought that maybe it would be better for everyone if you weren't here anymore. I still hate myself for thinking it, though I no longer hate you for making me think it.

When we were considering what to put on your headstone, I came up with something that I thought you'd like: *A pain in the ass who was deeply loved by many.* Mom shot down that idea, but I still think it rings true.

For years, I thought that love would be enough, but as much as we loved you, the trouble never stopped. Even long after your funeral, I got a call from a collection agency that was trying to track you down. (Don't worry, I told them you couldn't come to the phone right now.)

You knew how I felt about adopting you, but I'm not sure how you felt about being adopted. Don't get me wrong: I know you loved us and I'm sure that you knew that we loved you. But the adoption part was tricky. Adoption came with an asterisk, one with sharp points that cut deep.

When you were a little boy, the topic made you angry, and as an adult, you just shut it down. You never showed any interest in meeting your biological parents. Maybe that was because you were happy that we were your folks or maybe it hurt too much to think about them, I'll never know. All I know is that I never thought about you as my *adopted* son. You were just my son, I was just your dad, and that's just the way it was.

I don't know if you were "around," but I was in New York not long ago with Mom and Zach, and the three of us went to visit you in the cemetery. (Did you know that your headstone is right behind a guy named Eugene Levy?) After that, we drove to Huntington Harbor, where Mom had chartered a private boat. Its name was *Too Happy*, and so were we. We were supposedly celebrating both Mom's sixtieth birthday and Father's Day, but it was really just about us being together again.

It was a beautiful morning, and we had a great time cruising around the North Shore of Long Island. It was too early for cocktails, but we said fuck it and each grabbed a beer. "To Rob," we toasted.

About an hour in, the boat anchored, and we clambered out to the bow with a woman who was onboard to guide us through a meditation. I don't think we could've done this at any other time in our lives, but at that moment it seemed like the perfect thing to do. We rolled out yoga mats, did some movement and breathing exercises, and then she asked us to lie down and close our eyes.

She told us to imagine ourselves somewhere relaxing and beautiful, right before sunrise, and I immediately saw myself on a beach, watching waves gently break on the shore. Then she told us to picture ourselves in the middle of a circle, surrounded by the people we love.

Wherever I looked, I saw your face.

There you were with Mom sucking on a baby bottle, there you were in the bathtub rocking a shampoo Mohawk, and there was little Robbie, wearing a beanie and parka, holding a snowball. I kept looking around the circle and saw you sitting in a tree in our backyard in Woodbury, and then there you were with your arm around Zach's shoulders when you guys were teenagers. There you were again in my house in Venice with Zach on Christmas a few years ago, the last happy day the three of us had together. And then there at the beach, a few weeks before you died, were you and I—the sand and the water—looking out at the ocean for the last time.

I have a space in my heart that never closes.

You uttered those words when you were four, and now, at sixty-eight, I find myself saying them every day. I love you, Robbie James Carlat, and after all the bullshit and heartache, after the sleepless nights waiting for the inevitable phone call, and now despite the pain of living in the world without you, I will go to my grave (not too soon, I hope) convinced that adopting you was the best thing I ever did. If I had to go through all of it again, I'd do it in a heartbeat—the heartbeat that connects the two of us forever.

Peace out,
Dad

Acknowledgments

$\mathcal{I}$ didn't write this book alone. Rob was by my side in spirit, and there were many others who helped along the way.

Beginning at the beginning, there would be no book without my agent and friend, Angela Rinaldi—the most passionate advocate a writer could dream of—who deftly and patiently guided me to the finish line.

Thanks are also due to the wonderful people at Rowman & Littlefield, principally Jacquie Flynn, who (despite my pestering) meticulously shepherded this book into the world.

I am greatly indebted to many amazing folks at Our House Grief Support Center, particularly Jory Goldman, Maggi Wright, Irwin Feinberg, and Rachel Brenner, who taught me everything I know about "holding space," and to Marilyn Fleiss, my grief group coleader.

Special shoutouts to my editors at *Esquire*, Scott Omelianuk and Kelly Stout, two of the kindest and most thoughtful people I've ever had the pleasure of working with. And to Sarah Branham and Kevin Haynes, both brilliant editors as well as friends, who smoothed out the rough spots in early drafts of this book, making me appear smarter than I really am.

I am eternally grateful to have the two best friends in the world, Tony Gervino, who read countless manuscripts, gave great notes, and suggested I cut out profanity each and every time, and John Birmingham, who has edited every word I've ever written for the past forty years (including what you're reading right now) and has made my writing infinitely better, to say nothing of his compassionate and sound counsel. I love you, guys!

A big thank-you to the many kindhearted readers—you know who you are—who were generous with their time and gave me 92 percent positive feedback on the Larry Rotten Tomatoes meter, especially my little sister, Patti, who has always been my number one fan.

To Caryn, Zach, and Maura: we've been through a lot together and you will always have my unconditional love.

And last but by no means least, to Janie, who fills the space in my heart every single day.

About the Author

Larry Carlat is a writer and editor, whose work has appeared in the *New York Times Magazine*, *Esquire*, *GQ*, *Rolling Stone*, *Men's Journal*, *Men's Health*, and *Slam*. He is also a grief coach (www.griefforguys.com; larry@griefforguys.com) and volunteer group leader for bereaved parents at Our House Grief Support Center in Los Angeles and a member of its board of directors. He lives in Venice, California, with his significant other, Jane Evans, and their dog, Joe.